VICTORIAN PORCELAIN

THE VICTORIAN COLLECTOR SERIES

General Editor: HUGH WAKEFIELD
Keeper of the Department of Circulation, Victoria and Albert Museum

VICTORIAN LACE by Patricia Wardle
VICTORIAN PORCELAIN by Geoffrey A. Godden
VICTORIAN COSTUME by Anne M. Buck
VICTORIAN EMBROIDERY by Barbara Morris
VICTORIAN POTTERY by Hugh Wakefield
VICTORIAN SILVER AND SILVER-PLATE by Patricia Wardle

VICTORIAN PORCELAIN

By

GEOFFREY A. GODDEN
F.R.S.A.

FOREWORD BY HUGH WAKEFIELD
Keeper of the Department of Circulation, Victoria and Albert Museum

UNIVERSE BOOKS
New York

Published in the United States of America in 1970
by Universe Books
381 Park Avenue South, New York, N.Y. 10016

Previously distributed in the U.S. by Thomas Nelson & Sons

© Geoffrey A. Godden, 1961

All rights reserved. No part of this publication may be reproduced, stored in a retrieval system, or transmitted, in any form or by any means, electronic, mechanical, photocopying, recording, or otherwise, without the prior permission of the publishers.

ISBN 0 87663 126 X

Printed in Great Britain

FOREWORD

By

HUGH WAKEFIELD

Keeper of the Department of Circulation, Victoria and Albert Museum

INCREASINGLY the attention of collectors is being attracted to the Victorian decorative arts. This is partly because the quantity of surviving objects is far greater than those from earlier times; and partly because, with the passage of time, Victorian objects have ceased to be merely old-fashioned and are gradually coming to be assessed without prejudice as manifestations of the culture and outlook of an important period in history.

The art history of the period is, however, immensely complex, and the student of the Victorian decorative arts is easily tempted into the byways of quaint or bizarre trivialities. The books in the Victorian Collector Series represent a serious attempt on the part of the Editor and the various authors to present information which is based directly upon the study of Victorian objects and contemporary Victorian accounts of them, rather than upon unsubstantiated secondary sources.

Mr. Geoffrey Godden is well known to those who are already interested in the study of nineteenth-century porcelain. During the past ten years he has built up a personal collection of unique interest, which has been drawn upon for many of the illustrations in this volume. In this account of Victorian porcelain he presents a great deal of new information which comes from factory records and contemporary sources as well as from his own wide experience as a collector.

AUTHOR'S PREFACE

THE object of this volume is to give a general survey of the main English porcelain factories of the period and to illustrate their range of productions with photographs of both documentary and prosaic specimens. The illustrations, the majority of which have not previously been published, have been chosen to show the variety and the quality of the Victorian wares and to give some indication of the wide scope offered to collectors and students in this hitherto neglected field.

In the text, emphasis has been placed on the ceramic artists of the period, many of whom were attracted to England from the major continental factories by the relative prosperity of the English manufacturers. Alphabetical lists of the principal artists employed by each of the important factories are given under the relevant chapters.

The author makes no apologies for his extensive use of quotations from contemporary sources, as it is only by the use of these that statements that might otherwise be regarded as dogmatic can be confirmed as authoritative. In this respect the student of Victorian ceramics is much luckier than his colleague specialising in eighteenth-century porcelain who, having so little contemporary information at his disposal, must seek the aid of the scientist and the chemist to support his theories. Contemporary quotations are acknowledged in full. All line engravings are taken from the *Art Union* or *Art Journal* magazines.

The lists of factory marks should help in the identification and dating of Victorian porcelain. A number of hitherto unrecorded marks are included and these have been specially drawn from specimens in the author's collection. In particular the publication of many factory date cyphers should be of value to collectors and students. Every effort has been made to ascribe the correct dates to the ceramic artists mentioned in this volume, but it will be found that in many cases these dates differ from those given by previous writers.

Now that the best wares of the eighteenth century are becoming difficult to find and to buy an increasing interest is being taken by collectors in the wares of the Victorian period. While some of the pieces in the author's collection have been bought from leading dealers or from the great London auction galleries, many of his most prized documentary pieces have come cheaply from small second-hand shops and have cost but a few shillings.

The author is always grateful to receive information concerning Victorian ceramic artists or particulars of signed and dated examples of their work. Much hitherto unpublished material has been acquired through correspondence with ceramic artists or their families, and it is hoped that further information may be forthcoming from similar sources as a result of the publication of this book.

CONTENTS

	Page
Foreword by Hugh Wakefield	5
Author's Preface	7
Acknowledgements	15

Chapter

1.	The International Exhibitions	19
2.	Coalport	31
3.	Copeland	47
4.	Derby	68
5.	Minton	89
6.	Worcester	120
7.	The Parian Body	147
8.	*Pâte-sur-pâte*	170
9.	The Smaller Factories	189
10.	Notes on Dating	209
	Appendix I	212
	Appendix II	214
	Selected Bibliography	215
	Index	217

LIST OF PLATES

Plate		Page
1. COALPORT jug made for Queen Victoria		33
2. COALPORT plate—Emperor of Russia service		33
3. COALPORT vase—rococo		34
4. COALPORT vases—a pair by Randall and Cook		35
5. COALPORT dish painted by John Randall		35
6. COALPORT cup and saucer. 1851 Exhibition		36
7. COALPORT dish—classical subject		36
8. COALPORT vase painted by Cook		37
9. COALPORT vase—1862 Exhibition, by Abraham		37
10. COALPORT vases—a pair—studies by Randall		38
11. COALPORT vase—panel by Simpson		38
12. COPELAND & GARRETT floral plate by Evans		55
13. COPELAND & GARRETT fireplace panels		56
14. COPELAND & GARRETT greyhound		56
15. COPELAND Sèvres style vase. 1851 Exhibition		57
16. COPELAND ewer—scenic panel by Lucas		58
17. COPELAND vase Turner subject by Lucas		58
18. COPELAND vase decorated by C. F. Hürten		59
19. COPELAND vase painted by Besche		59
20. COPELAND plaque painted by C. F. Hürten		59
21. COPELAND vase decorated by S. Alcock		60
22. COPELAND plaque painted by W. Yale		61
23. COPELAND "Jewelled" plate painted by S. Alcock		61
24. DERBY plaque painted by John Haslem		62
25. DERBY plaque decorated in the Sèvres style		63
26. STEVENSON & HANCOCK figures—a pair		63
27. DERBY traditional "Japan" patterns		64
28. DERBY vase, yellow ground		64
29. DERBY plate painted by J. Rouse		81

ILLUSTRATIONS

Plate   *Page*

30. DERBY vase decorated by D. Leroy 81
31. MINTON oval portrait plaque by J. Simpson . . . 82
32. MINTON vase painted rose studies by J. Smith . . 82
33. MINTON coloured parian figures—a pair . . . 82
34. MINTON vase in the Sèvres style painted by Allen . . 83
35. MINTON vase—figure subjects by T. Allen . . . 83
36. MINTON plate, cupid subjects by T. Kirkby . . . 84
37. MINTON plate 1851 Exhibition scenic panel . . . 85
38. MINTON centrepiece designed by E. Jeannest . . . 85
39. MINTON vase, 1862 Exhibition 86
40. MINTON vase, 1862 Exhibition painted by L. Jahn . . 87
41. MINTON vase, 1862 Exhibition painted by T. Allen . . 87
42. MINTON imitation of a Chinese vase by L. Arnoux . . 88
43. MINTON plate—figure subject design by W. S. Coleman 105
44. MINTON vase painted by A. Boullemier 105
45. MINTON *seau* decorated in white enamel by D. Leroy . 106
46. MINTON plate—painted by A. H. Wright . . . 106
47. MINTON plate painted by A. Boullemier . . . 107
48. MINTON copy of a Sèvres vase painted by L. Boullemier 107
49. CHAMBERLAIN WORCESTER vase 108
50. KERR & BINNS "Shakespeare" comport . . . 109
51. KERR & BINNS dish by T. Bott 110
52. KERR & BINNS dish by T. Bott 110
53. ROYAL WORCESTER *déjeuner* service—panels by J. Callowhill 111
54. ROYAL WORCESTER—the Ormond vase by Bott . . 112
55. ROYAL WORCESTER vase painted by J. Rushton . . 112
56. ROYAL WORCESTER Norman Conquest ewer and stand by Bott 129
57. ROYAL WORCESTER—Norman Conquest vase by Bott . 130
58. ROYAL WORCESTER Japanese style vase by Hadley . 130
59. ROYAL WORCESTER vase in the Japanese style . . 131
60. ROYAL WORCESTER the "Potter" vase by Hadley . 132
61. ROYAL WORCESTER vase in the Persian style . . 133

Plate	Page
62. ROYAL WORCESTER three "Kate Greenaway" style figures	133
63. ROYAL WORCESTER "ivory" nef by Hadley	134
64. ROYAL WORCESTER gilt vase, Louis XVI style	134
65. GEORGE OWEN at work on his carved wares	135
66. WORCESTER dish decorated by George Sparks	135
67. "HADLEY" vase, floral pattern	136
68. GRAINGER WORCESTER vase and cover painted by J. Stinton	136
69. COPELAND PARIAN figure "Narcissus"	153
70. MINTON PARIAN group "Una and the Lion"	154
71. MINTON PARIAN figure "Dorothea"	154
72. MINTON PARIAN figure "Mercury"	155
73. MINTON PARIAN figure "Miranda"	156
74. MINTON PARIAN "Naomi and her daughters-in-law"	156
75. MINTON PARIAN covered bowl, 1851 Exhibition	157
76. COPELAND PARIAN group—"Ino & Bacchus", 1851 Exhibition	158
77. KERR & BINNS PARIAN group—"Faust and Margaret"	158
78. ADAMS PARIAN group	159
79. MINTON PARIAN figure of Herbert Minton	159
80. PARIAN brooches	160
81. BELLEEK PARIAN ice-pail and cover	177
82. MINTON *pâte-sur-pâte* plate by L. Birks	178
83. MINTON *pâte-sur-pâte* vases—a pair by H. Hollins	179
84. MOORE *pâte-sur-pâte* vases—a pair by Sanders	179
85. GRAINGER *pâte-sur-pâte* vase by Locke	180
86. MINTON *pâte-sur-pâte* three apprentice pieces	181
87. G. JONES *pâte-sur-pâte* wall pockets by F. Schenck	181
88. MINTON *pâte-sur-pâte* plaque by Solon	182
89. MINTON *pâte-sur-pâte* vase by A. Birks	183
90. MINTON *pâte-sur-pâte* vase by A. Birks	184
91. MINTON *pâte-sur-pâte* vase by Solon	184
92. MINTON *pâte-sur-pâte* vases by Solon	185

Plate *Page*

93. DAVENPORT jug dated 1856 186
94. MOORE clock case 203
95. MOORE centrepiece painted by Pilsbury . . . 204
96. DOULTON vase by G. White 204
97. RIDGWAY, BATES scenic plate 205
98. DOULTON porcelain plate 206
99. Signed plaque by JESSE MOUNTFORD . . . 207
100. Signed plaque by WILLIAM CORDEN 207
101. Signed plaque by T. SIMPSON 208
102. Signed plaque by JOHN RANDALL 208

ACKNOWLEDGEMENTS

THE author acknowledges with gratitude the valuable assistance accorded to him by the various manufacturers. In particular he is grateful to the late Mr. J. Steel, Curator of the Minton Works Museum, and his successor Mr. F. G. Taylor; also to Mr. Cyril Shingler, Curator of the Worcester Works Museum, Mr. J. W. Upsdell of W. T. Copeland & Sons, Mr. C. F. Osborn of the Royal Crown Derby Porcelain Co. and Mr. F. W. Kerry of the Doulton Fine China Co.

Considerable help and encouragement has been given by Mr. Geoffrey Bemrose, Curator of the Hanley Museum and Art Gallery, by the officials of the Victoria & Albert Museum, particularly Mr. Hugh Wakefield, Keeper of the Department of Circulation (the General Editor of this series), and by the modern ceramic historian Mr. Reginald G. Haggar.

Acknowledgements are also due to the *Pottery Gazette and Glass Trade Review*, Cassell & Co. (*The Magazine of Art*), Hulton Press (*Studio*) and to the Hutchinson Group (*Staffordshire Pots and Potters* by G. W. & F. A. Rhead). Information kindly supplied by relatives of many of the Victorian ceramic artists has been incorporated in this work and the author regrets that it is not practicable to acknowledge fully the help given by these individuals.

The following have kindly given permission for the reproduction of illustrations and marks: W. T. Copeland & Sons, Doulton & Co., Mintons, the Worcester Royal Porcelain Co., the Victoria & Albert Museum, the Hove Museum & Art Gallery and the Conservatoire National des Arts et Métiers, Paris. Where illustrations are not acknowledged they are of specimens in the author's collection The author is also indebted to Mr. Donald Abbott, F.R.S.A., for his careful drawing of the marks.

Acknowledgements of a more personal nature are due to my father for putting my notes into readable form and to Derek Gardiner, A.I.B.P., for posing and photographing many of the pieces illustrated.

VICTORIAN PORCELAIN

CHAPTER 1

THE INTERNATIONAL EXHIBITIONS

THE many international exhibitions held during the nineteenth century are of great importance to the student of Victorian decorative arts, for not only did the manufacturers produce especially ambitious specimens for their stands, but these were described, and in many cases illustrated, in the various guides, catalogues and reviews. Furthermore many of these exhibition pieces were purchased for national and provincial museums and are thus preserved and available for study.

In this chapter, which may be regarded as a general introduction to Victorian ceramic art, the reader may follow the main trends of the ceramic fashions of the period as portrayed in the contemporary exhibition reviews. These developments in taste are not always apparent in the chapters dealing with the individual factories as, in many cases, traditional styles were so popular that they were continued in spite of changing fashions.

Although pride of place as the most completely documented record of the production of the period must go to "The Great Exhibition of the Works of Industry of all Nations" usually known as the 1851 Exhibition, various small local exhibitions were of earlier date. In particular those held at Manchester in 1845–6 and at Birmingham in 1849 were of considerable interest and both were reviewed in the *Art Union* magazine.

The *Art Union*'s report of the 1845–6 Manchester Exhibition of British Industrial Art is mainly confined to the products of Copeland & Garrett (see Chapter 3) and is here quoted at length as it is the first comprehensive account we have of the wares shown by one of the leading ceramic manufacturers in a Victorian exhibition "The stand, devoted to the productions of Messrs. Copeland & Garrett occupies the whole centre of the small exhibition room, it is so arranged as to display to advantage the various works, which consist of porcelain slabs of very large dimensions adapted for fireplaces, panels for furniture, tops for tables, drawing-room or toilet etc. ornamental vases for gardens, conservatories etc. statuettes, pompeiian copies, parts of dinner services, dessert services, breakfast services, together with the common printed plates, common only because of the cheap rate at which they are produced. . . . The visitors to the Exposition will be first struck by the exceeding beauty of the flower painting. . . . The delicacy and beauty of the art is most apparent in a table top with groups and festoons of flowers. Near it are two small landscapes in circular frames, exquisitely painted. . . . These are the productions of AN ARTIST—one who would have achieved excellence while mastering any material. Among the dessert plates, those are the most striking and original which exhibit wreaths of various kinds or orchidaeus plants, and passion flowers and hearts-ease. . . . There were also two or three subjects of figures of animals deserving of remark; one in particular of fox hounds was treated with peculiar and excellent effect. Of inkstands, there are three . . . one surmounted by a Cupid, one of white and gold and one which is named the Louis Inkstand." The report continues: "The Pompeiian 'Mortuary' vases, always so exquisite in form, have supplied many valuable hints to this establishment. Suggestions have been obtained from this rich and fertile source, not only for ornaments of the more costly class, but for matter of daily use . . . witness the ewers and bowls for chamber services, which have been subjected to various decorations, all in good taste. Apt aids have been borrowed, also, from the tartans of the several Scottish clans. Flower painting on porcelain has been brought to very high perfection by the artists of this establishment . . . some of the flower pieces on Copeland and Garrett's stall are painted in very subdued tones, and have not only the natural appearance of flowers seen behind sunshine . . . but have the suggestive force of calling imagination into action to explain the atmospheric haze, which actually reveals, while it seems to hide, the beauty of the floral group. . . . " Copeland & Garrett's new statuary porcelain, or parian, figures were also praised in this early review (see Chapter 7).

An original *Art Union* engraving of Copeland and Garrett's stand at Manchester is reproduced on page 21.

In the years 1847, 1848 and 1849, the Society of Arts organised a series of small exhibitions in London. In the ceramic sections the emphasis was on the newly introduced parian body, and, during 1847 and 1848, on the models displayed by "Summerly's Art

Manufactures". The latter was a short-lived endeavour to combine the talents of leading artists with the manufacturing ability of the foremost producers. This venture will receive further notice in Chapter 9.

The Birmingham Exhibition of 1849 followed much the pattern of that in Manchester two years earlier. The Copeland firm, which was known as W. T. Copeland and Sons from 1847 continued to exhibit their statuary porcelain, or parian, and their porcelain slabs richly decorated for fireplace panels and for table tops. Mintons exhibited a "a large variety of objects of every order of porcelain: statuettes, vases, dessert plates, articles of elegant utility or of luxurious decoration exercising the purest and best taste in design and composed with exquisite beauty of workmanship" (*Art Journal*, 1849). Fine vases in an eighteenth-century Sèvres style were also shown on the Mintons' stand.

The 1851 exhibition held in Paxton's "Crystal Palace" in Hyde Park was the first truly international exhibition held in this country and the British manufacturers naturally strove to produce the most fabulous *tours de force* for the occasion. Many of these were illustrated in the catalogues and this has given rise to the mistaken idea that they are representative of the typical productions of the period, whereas they are in fact purely exhibition pieces, the production of which would have been uneconomic for commercial purposes. The normal productions of the period were well represented in the exhibition but received scant notice in the catalogues. Mintons, for instance, exhibited "a variety of teacups and saucers, dessert and dinner plates, and *déjeûne* sets" and it is to such pieces that we must look if we are to get a proper appreciation of the styles and taste of the period. Plate 6 illustrates a Coalport example picked at random from the collection at the Conservatoire National des Arts et Métiers in Paris. This was bought at the 1851 Exhibition and is surprisingly modest.

The following extracts, unless otherwise stated, are taken from the official Juries Reports, and provide an overall picture of the products of the main porcelain manufacturers exhibiting in 1851. Mintons of Stoke-on-Trent were said to "stand foremost among the British exhibitors for the number, variety and beauty of their articles . . . the articles exhibited by Messrs. Minton in imitation of old Sèvres, their flower paintings on a great variety of plates, on their small tea services, on their earthenware basins, ewers, etc., and on their smaller articles of a more purely decorative character are all remarkable for great freshness of effect and excellent taste". Parian figures and vases were also shown in considerable variety, together with earthenware fireplace slabs, tiles and garden furniture in terra cotta and majolica.

A further account of Mintons' exhibits is given by Ralph Nicholson Wornum in his paper "The Exhibition as a lesson in taste" incorporated in the *Art Journal*'s Catalogue of the Exhibition: "Minton and Co. . . . make likewise a magnificent display, especially in a dessert service in parian and porcelain mixing, in turquoise, white and gold, purchased by Her Majesty. On this stall is a beautiful Cinquecento ewer and basin, in parian, which is one of the most tasteful specimens of this class of design in the Exhibition. . . . This firm exhibits also a pair of magnificent vases, of which the handles, in metal, are extremely beautiful . . . and there are also some clever imitations in Parian of the delicate trifles of old Dresden china, in flowers and fancy figures, of the school of Watteau. The colours generally and the ordinary services of this firm, are extremely good, and its encaustic tiles are a very important contribution towards the general cultivation of taste. . . . The Louis Quinze is still the prevailing style in porcelain, as in many other manufactures, and, generally speaking, profusion of ornament is the rule."

The Louis Quinze or Sèvres taste was certainly the prevailing style. Of seventeen porcelain vases, or pairs of vases, on Mintons' stand no less than fifteen were acknowledged to be after old Sèvres models.

The Coalport factory (John Rose & Co.) showed fine dessert services mainly in the Sèvres style. The original ground colours were closely imitated and the painting included reserve panels by William Cook (flowers) and John Randall (birds). Figure groups, clock-cases and epergnes were shown in parian ware.

As may be expected, Copelands who had introduced the parian body some six years earlier made a great display of this "statuary porcelain" based on designs and originals by the best known sculptors of the day. "This exhibition [the Copeland stand] is remarkable in several respects, especially for the great beauty of its parian groups and figures, several of which are eminently successful, and show complete mastery over this material in its best and most legitimate application." Besides jewelled, gilt and painted services, the firm had specialised in porcelain and earthenware fireplace panels and tables. "The Jury especially desire to mention the large porcelain slabs or panels decorated with flower-painting and other patterns, and now much used for fireplaces, panels, tables . . . the large flower-painting on some of these has a very handsome effect." The artists who were employed on these large panels included David Evans, the flower painter and Daniel Lucas the scenic artist.

Wornum in his paper emphasises the extent to which the classical mode of decoration was favoured by Copelands. "We have in this stall much of the variation of classical models which appears to us to constitute the true use of these ancient remains and the best evidence of a refined taste. There is besides on this stall much handsome porcelain of modern design, rich in decoration, without being gaudy; and, in several styles, all well expressed, as the Indian, Moorish, Cinquecento, and the Louis Quatorze, and Louis Quinze; but the Greek justly prevails over all the others."

The City of Worcester was represented by the firms of Chamberlain and G. Grainger. Chamberlains showed samples of "pierced or honey-comb china", porcelain plaques, vases, baskets, dessert and dinner ware as well as "china bracelets and brooches, china mortice door-furniture", but their display fell short of the high standards associated with earlier Worcester porcelain. This fact was recognised by the management and was the cause of the new Kerr & Binns Company being formed in 1852. This developed in

1862 into the Worcester Royal Porcelain Company which still flourishes to-day (see Chapter 6). G. Grainger's display included dinner and dessert wares, an openwork coffee service and examples of their new semi-porcelain and parian bodies.

Other firms exhibiting at the Great Exhibition included Samuel Alcock (wares decorated with figure subjects in relief); T. & R. Boote (parian vases and figures); G. F. Bowers (porcelain and earthenware); J. Clementson (earthenware); E. Deakin (silver lustre earthenware); Charles Mason (ironstone china); T. J. & J. Mayer (earthenware); Charles Meigh (porcelain, earthenware and parian); F. & R. Pratt (colour-printed earthenware); John Ridgway (porcelain and earthenware); Josiah Wedgwood and Sons (jasper and other traditional wares). Several decorating firms were also represented, including that of John Wager Brameld of Bayswater who is better known for his previous associations with the Rockingham works.

The Dublin Exhibition of 1853 provided the newly formed Worcester firm, Kerr & Binns, with the first opportunity of showing its wares. The most ambitious of these was a dessert service which included centrepieces with parian figure groups inspired by Shakespeare's *A Midsummer Night's Dream* (Plate 50). In the same exhibition Copelands showed a selection of their statuary porcelain (parian) and decorative fireplace panels; and A. B. & R. P. Daniell, the retailing firm, showed Coalport porcelain consisting mainly of vases in Sèvres style decorated with floral, bird and figure panels.

In 1855 the English manufacturers were able to compete with their continental rivals at the Paris Universal Exhibition. "The sale of Minton and Copeland's porcelain has long been very considerable, and within a few days the Worcester manufactory has received large orders, including some thousands of pieces of its famous egg shell porcelain" (*Art Journal*, 1855). The Coalport factory sent a number of figure-supported parian comports and centrepieces with a dessert service. "This service is one of the most magnificent productions in porcelain ever manufactured in England . . . the ground is of turquoise blue, the evenness and brilliancy of which are very remarkable; the plates are painted from the compositions of Watteau, and are pencilled and coloured with the utmost delicacy and finish" (*Art Journal*, 1855). Copelands made their usual feature of parian figures: ". . . the leading objects are those figures, groups, vases etc. of statuary porcelain, which have so greatly raised the repute of this establishment, giving it, indeed, renown throughout Europe. But the admiration excited is by no means confined to those productions; the painted vases, more especially those which imitate gems, or are in low relief, are in all respects, of the very highest excellence" (*Art Journal*, 1855). The Kerr & Binns' display was noteworthy, for at Paris in 1855 we find the first exhibition reference to their "Limoges" enamels which were later to become one of the best known products of the factory. "Messrs. Kerr and Binns of Worcester show a few fine examples of their productions of Limoges ware—which show very distinctly how far the attention of the porcelain painters of the present day may be successfully directed to the rivalry of the best and most refined works of a past age" (*Art Journal*, 1855).

The 1862 International Exhibition held in London is, after the 1851 exhibition, the best documented, owing to the publication of three volumes of *Masterpieces of Industrial Art and Sculpture at the International Exhibition* chosen and described by J. B. Waring.

The Coalport wares shown by their London agents, A. B. & R. P. Daniell, included Sèvres-type vases with coloured grounds and finely painted panels by R. F. Abraham, J. Birkbeck, W. Cook and J. Rouse. A single vase painted by Abraham was valued at £125 (Plate 9). Copelands showed for the first time the fine floral painting of C. F. Hürten whose work was to be included in every later exhibition up to the time of his retirement in 1897. A large vase over four feet high painted by Hürten was bought for the South Kensington Museum. This vase was cast in a mould seven feet high involving the use of over a ton of plaster. Of more ordinary objects we read in Waring's *Masterpieces* "some of the prettiest pieces in the Exhibition were to be seen in Mr. Copeland's case . . . consisting of small vases of very pure form enwreathed with violets, roses, convulvuli, etc., on a white ground. Mr. Copeland's landscape subjects were also exceedingly good. A great deal of very good parian Statuary from models by Foley, Marshall Wood, Noble and other well known sculptors reproducing their best works in a very beautiful material, obtainable at a price which brings them within the reach of the general public."

Besides their interesting earthenware Mintons were showing ornate porcelain vases of Sèvres type painted with figure subjects by L. Jahn and T. Allen. Waring states that "Great variety and good taste were observable in the porcelain contributed by this firm but we were struck with a super-abundance to our minds, of old Sèvres models." The retailing firm of Thomas Goode showed a Minton dessert service valued at £1000 which included a wealth of elaborate figure-supported comports in porcelain and parian.

The 1862 Exhibition marked the end of the Kerr & Binns period of Worcester porcelain and the birth of the Worcester Royal Porcelain Company. The last products of the Kerr & Binns period were shown and included a service made for Queen Victoria and painted by Thomas Bott. A plate from this service is preserved in the Victoria and Albert Museum. Parian, "Raphaelesque" porcelain and finely ornamented specimens in oxidised silver, gold and bronze were also shown. "The enamel paintings, for which this firm has obtained the highest reputation were unsurpassed by any in the Exhibition. The small vases, tazzas, etc., ornamented with medallions containing coloured portraits on a gold ground, the body of each piece being of a very delicate turquoise blue, 'bleu de roi' and sometimes simply white, were peculiarly pleasing and attractive, both regards form and colour" (*Waring*).

The Paris Exhibition of 1867 included contributions by Mintons, Copelands and Worcester. Referring to Mintons' porcelain the *Art Journal* said: "Figure subjects, landscapes and flowers are rendered with equal skill, and with the highest finish in all their details. . . . These paintings too are remarkable for the delicacy and transparency of their colours."

Besides a notable display of earthenware "majolica", their other exhibits included parian figures, groups and centrepieces as well as a fine white porcelain chandelier. On the Copeland stand the most attractive feature was Hürten's flower painting. "Messrs. Copeland's artists direct their attention chiefly to flower painting. If, however, Messrs. Copeland had contributed nothing to the exhibition beyond the magnificent dessert service made for the Prince of Wales, they would well have maintained their ground against all foreign rivalry" (*Art Journal*, 1867). This service was decorated with floral panels painted by Hürten and comprised elaborate figure-supported centrepieces, wine coolers and comports. The Royal Worcester Company's display included their now celebrated Limoges enamels painted by Thomas Bott. They also showed jewelled porcelain, and among this was a magnificent tête-à-tête service made for presentation to the Countess of Dudley. Some duplicate pieces of this service, which are preserved in the Worcester Works Museum are illustrated in Plate 53.

Exhibitions were held in London in 1871, 1872, 1873 and 1874. In general the exhibits were similar to those shown at Paris in 1867. The innovations at this period were Solon's early masterpieces of *pâte-sur-pâte* decoration and the Worcester wares in the Japanese taste, both of which will later be dealt with in detail. In the 1867 Exhibition the Irish Belleek Company exhibited wares in forms based on marine motifs—a style of decoration which was to become traditionally associated with the name of Belleek. Copelands' statuary porcelain or parian continued in popularity and it is interesting to see that the 1851 Exhibition group "Ino and Bacchus" (Plate 76) was included again in the 1871 Exhibition.

At the Universal Exhibition of 1873 held in Vienna, English ceramic wares were well represented. The *Art Journal* contributor wrote: "Within the precincts of the Exhibition at Vienna there is not any collective display of pottery, china or porcelain, which at all approaches that sent by the manufacturers of England in quality of material, variety of glaze, good modelling, decorative enrichment by enamel painting and uniformly good finish." Copelands were quickly following the Worcester lead in the Japanese taste and showed dessert sets and ornate vases in this style at Vienna. At this period R. F. Abraham was the Art Director and was himself a well-known ceramic artist formerly employed at Coalport. Two new Copeland artists are mentioned in the accounts of this Exhibition—L. Besche, a figure painter from Mintons, and J. Weaver, Senr., a painter of birds. The Minton exhibits included Solon's *pâte-sur-pâte*. "Both for execution and design M. Solon is to be complimented on his artistic success, and that we were not singular in our opinion is proved by the fact that many of the series (of plaques) have been purchased both by the Berlin and the Buda-Pest Art Museums; some even will have to travel to the Massachusetts Museum at Boston" (*Art Journal*, 1873). Mintons' painted wares were by Thomas Allen, Henry Mitchell and William Mussill. In the Worcester section were displayed the last works of Thomas Bott, together with examples of the firm's jewelled wares. The Worcester porcelain in the Japanese style imitating carved ivory, bronze and gold, was perhaps the most significant of all the English work in the exhibition.

At the Paris Exhibition of 1878 the English manufacturers

exhibited in force and the following description of this Exhibition is taken from a most interesting, but little known, account written by George Augustus Sala and published in two volumes under the title *Paris Herself Again* (1879). Describing the Minton exhibits, Sala gave pride of place to Solon's *pâte-sur-pâte* (his remarks on this are quoted in Chapter 8) and continued: "Passing to other exhibits in porcelain, much and admiring interest has been taken in the 'Prometheus Vases' in turquoise; the handsome vases with cupids by Boullemier, after Angelica Kauffman (purchased by Queen Victoria) the dessert plates of 'bleu du roi' painted with subjects from Molière's plays, a 'Rose du Barri' vase, and plates of 'gros bleu' in the old Sèvres style, painted with subjects after Boucher. There are, moreover, perforated trays, with paintings after Teniers, some exquisitely enamelled vases in the Japanese cloisonné manner, and several fine reproductions in underglaze majolica of celebrated portraits by Sir Joshua Reynolds. The skilful reproductions of the Piron or Henri Deux ware are well worthy of notice, as are also the 'faiences' in the Indian and Persian style, and a colossal vase, upheld by cupids, graduating apparently for athletes, in turquoise and gold Persian ware, of rare refinement and finish."

Referring to the Worcester collection Sala remarked: "Varied as the collection altogether is, many of the more recent productions indicate in a decided manner the art influence of Japan; still it is not so much the spirit of slavish imitation that is apparent as the judicious adaptation of the more graceful forms and higher styles of ornamentation in vogue among the aesthetic and skilful Orientals." He considered however that: "Unquestionably the most important objects displayed by the famous Worcester establishment are the pair of large vases in the Renaissance style, ornamented with delicately modelled bas-reliefs in richly framed compartments on their sides." One of these vases which illustrate various ceramic pursuits is shown in Plate 60.

Of Copelands' contribution to this exhibition Sala wrote: "I should be blind, indeed, were I insensible to the merit of this charming gathering of porcelain, comprising as it does, a series of beautiful plaques in blue monochrome of well known gems of English landscape scenery; a number of vases of Japanese character ... four tasteful paintings of the Seasons on an earthenware ground, a delicious plaque of a Spanish boy, after Murillo; and a number of graceful and refined statuettes, including the famous 'Sleep of Sorrow and Dream of Joy' in the snowy-white ware for the production of which Messrs. Copeland have been so long and so deservedly celebrated. These, with a number of delicate 'tazze' 'jardinièrs' and vases, and a charming 'déjeûner' set in 'jewelled' porcelain—the ground being enriched by minute gems representing rubies, pearls, emeralds and turquoise, set in subtly fanciful patterns, make up a cabinet of ceramic specimens unpretendingly but most adequately chronicling the development of the art of potter's skill during more than a century in England." Sala also wrote in glowing terms of the Doulton and Wedgwood wares, both outside the scope of the present volume. Among the smaller porcelain manufacturers mentioned by Sala was the firm of Brown-Westhead, Moore. "They are producers at first hand of some remarkably well executed vases and plaques, displaying rare beauty of form and brilliance of colour, and of a variety of quaintly designed flower-holders, in which birds and animals are felicitously introduced. . . ."

It is hoped that the reader will now have a general picture of the main trends of ceramic decoration during the Victorian era and that he may have formed some idea of the specialities of the major manufacturers. In the next five chapters the history and productions of these houses will be discussed in greater detail, their ceramic artists listed, and the marks illustrated.

INTERNATIONAL EXHIBITIONS OF THE VICTORIAN PERIOD

1851	The Great Exhibition, London.
1853	Dublin International Exhibition.
1855	Paris Universal Exhibition.
1862	London International Exhibition.
1865	Dublin International Exhibition.
1867	Paris Universal Exhibition.
1871 1872 1873 1874	South Kensington International Exhibitions.
1873	Vienna Universal Exhibition.
1876	Philadelphia Centennial Exhibition.
1878	Paris Universal Exhibition.
1887	Manchester, Royal Jubilee Exhibition.

1893　Chicago, World's Columbian Exhibition.
1900　Paris Universal Exhibition.
1900　Vienna Secession Exhibition.
1901　Glasgow International Exhibition.

Among local exhibitions those at Manchester (1845-6) and Birmingham (1849) are of particular interest in the history of the decorative arts.

MINTON LOUIS QUINZE CANDLESTICK FIGURE, 1851

CHAPTER 2

COALPORT: JOHN ROSE & Co.

COALPORT was not alone amongst the Victorian ceramic factories in owing a great deal to the standards and experience of previous eras. In 1799 John Rose, the proprietor of the Coalport factory, had purchased the Caughley works, where he had served his apprenticeship; and early in the nineteenth-century he bought up the moulds and stock-in-trade of the Swansea and Nantgarw factories. One direct result of the latter purchase was a great improvement in the Coalport body and glaze, and in 1820 Rose received a Society of Arts gold medal for the best lead-free glaze. A special self-explanatory mark was used on articles finished with this material.

At the beginning of the period under review the Coalport factory had already established itself as the foremost producer of the floral encrusted porcelain, which is usually known as Coalbrookdale but is also referred to as Colebrook-Dale in some contemporary notices. This style, with its strong rococo feeling, was to continue for many years and indeed influenced the whole range of the factory's productions. Vases, jugs and baskets richly adorned with naturalistic floral encrustation were made in great profusion. The floral painted jug illustrated in Plate 1 is a typical example of the rococo forms used and is part of a service made for Queen Victoria on her succession. At this period there is a decided similarity in style between the productions of Coalport and Rockingham, each factory seemingly endeavouring to out-do the other in rococo extravagance. Both factories made some charming small figures and groups, but these, like most of the early Coalport porcelain, were unmarked.

John Rose died in November 1841 and was succeeded by his nephew W. F. Rose, and William Pugh; and they, for a short period, were mainly content to continue the well-tried and successful floral encrusted wares and the widespread use of rococo forms. A few years later, however, we find the factory concentrating mainly on reviving the Sèvres style with its simpler forms decorated with rich ground colours and finely painted reserve panels. The technical improvements in the body and the successful experiments carried out to re-discover or imitate the rich Sèvres colours, were remarked upon in the *Art Journal* of 1849: ". . . our attention was called to the purity of the material entering into the composition of some white plates from the pottery of Rose & Co. . . . From the same house are several specimens of plates which are plainly ornamented with a simple band of colour, but these bands certainly indicate the large amount of chemical knowledge which has been employed in their production. Some of the blues, cobalt and others, are exceedingly pure and beautiful. . . ." Individual examples in the Sèvres taste had been produced by Coalport and other factories earlier in the century, but only to a limited extent.

By 1850 the Coalport factory was fully committed to its revival of the Sèvres style and the excellence of the productions of this period can be seen from documentary plates made for the Museum of Practical Geology. These plates are fully marked and dated 1850, and are now preserved in the Victoria & Albert Museum. In many cases original Sèvres models were copied so successfully that they were sold as genuine Sèvres and embellished with that factory's mark. The vase in the Jones collection at the Victoria & Albert Museum (No. 765-1882) is a classic example of this practice. The Minton and Copeland essays in the Sèvres style were usually clearly marked with the names of their respective manufacturers. Chelsea porcelain was also extensively copied at Coalport in this period and often bore a replica of the gold anchor mark. In some cases the styles were transposed—a Chelsea vase form might be decorated in the Sèvres style and the model shown in Plate 4 is an example of this.

The London retailers, A. B. & R. P. Daniell of Wigmore Street and New Bond Street, were closely connected with the Coalport firm, and showed Coalport wares under their own name in many international exhibitions. Many of the pieces were manufactured especially for this firm and marked with its name. No effort was spared to see that these imitations were as perfect as possible, and original Sèvres examples were even borrowed by Daniells for this purpose from the Royal Collection.

Of the many ground colours used at Coalport the richest was undoubtedly the *Bleu de Roi*, a dark, brilliant underglaze blue which can be seen to advantage on two of the Museum of Practical Geology plates. This colour was a perfect foil to the richly tooled gilding of the Sèvres-type productions. The so-called Rose du Barry, which is more properly called Rose Pompadour, was introduced about 1849

1

COALPORT jug, part of a service made for Queen Victoria. *c.* 1837. Ht. 6½ in. Mark No. 2.

2

COALPORT plate, part of a service presented by Queen Victoria to the Emperor of Russia in 1845. *Victoria & Albert Museum*.

3. COALPORT vase, a late example of the revived rococo style. *c.* 1850. Ht. 20⅛ in. *Victoria & Albert Museum.*

4
COALPORT vases in the Sèvres style, painted by J. Randall. William Cook's floral painting on reverse. *c.* 1850. Ht. 11 in. Mark No. 4.

5
COALPORT shaped dish decorated by John Randall in the Sèvres taste with fine tooled gilding. *c.* 1851. 5½ in. × 8½ in. Mark No. 5.

Page 35

6. COALPORT (John Rose & Co.) cup and saucer painted with floral sprays on a Rose du Barry ground. 1851 Exhibition. *Conservatoire National des Arts et Métiers, Paris.*

7. COALPORT footed dish decorated with classical figure subject in the style associated with R. F. Abraham. *c.* 1850. $6\frac{3}{4} \times 5\frac{1}{2}$ in. Mark No. 5.

8
COALPORT vase showing William Cook's floral and fruit compositions. *c.* 1860. Ht. 8½ in.

9
COALPORT vase and cover, the central panel painted by R. F. Abraham. 1862 Exhibition. Ht. 30 in. Mark No. 6.

Page 37

10

COALPORT vases, each bearing three panels of J. Randall's bird studies. 1871 Exhibition. Ht. 17 in. Mark No. 6.

11

COALPORT vase, the scenic panel painted by Percy Simpson. c. 1900. Ht. 11½ in. Mark No. 9.

Page 38

and was much praised at the 1851 Exhibition. This colour was used extensively over a long period. Two greens were used, a deep rich Sardinian shade and the lighter Victorian green. The pale turquoise called Celeste was not as successful as the other colours. The maroon ground had been introduced as early as 1821, and all the ground colours mentioned above were in use in time to be featured in the 1851 Exhibition.

The copies of Sèvres porcelain with their panels of exotic birds and floral compositions could not have been made without the assistance of skilled painters to decorate them. An experienced painter of birds in the Sèvres style was John Randall (b. 1810, d. 1910). At the age of eighteen, he was apprenticed to his uncle, Thomas Martin Randall, and was trained to decorate in the Sèvres style. T. M. Randall decorated, or rather re-decorated, a considerable quantity of English and French porcelain in the Sèvres manner at his London workshop and later at his small factory at Madeley. Much of this re-decorated ware was genuine Sèvres porcelain and bore the original mark, but was sparsely painted, inexpensive and generally of an unsaleable type before Randall enriched it with delicate ground colours containing reserve panels of Watteau-style figures, exotic birds and flowers in the most fashionable manner. John Randall left Madeley and worked at Rockingham for two years. In 1835 he joined the Coalport Company and continued to paint exotic birds in the Sèvres manner as he had been accustomed to do at Madeley and at the Rockingham factory. So successful were Randall's copies of Sèvres porcelain that an example of his work was bought unknowingly by his Managing Director, Rose, as a genuine example and returned to the factory for Randall to copy. The 1850's and 60's marked the peak of Randall's painting in the Sèvres style. Later he turned to studies of birds in their natural surroundings (Plate 10). Although the Coalport artists were not allowed to sign their work until later in the century, "Randall's birds" became as famous in their day as had William Billingsley's roses a generation before. In 1881 John Randall retired from ceramic painting because of failing eyesight. In his later years he wrote several books; his *History of Madeley* and *Clay Industries* contain a wealth of information on the small Madeley factory and on the Coalport factory in the early nineteenth century. He had always taken a keen interest in geology and in 1863 was elected a Fellow of the Geological Society. His collection of minerals and fossils was included in the 1851 exhibition and was bought for the Nation. He died in 1910.

It will be noticed that many specimens of Randall's painting are on pieces which also include some colourful floral and fruit painting. A plate, for instance, might have Randall birds in the centre with border panels of fruit and flowers; or a vase might have birds on one side and flowers on the reverse. The artist responsible for floral and fruit decoration was William Cook, who, like Randall, had received his early training at the Madeley works. Cook who joined the Coalport factory about 1840 was employed over a long period. His floral compositions always display a bright palette, often blending fruit and flowers happily together. A *Pottery Gazette* (1890) writer noted, "William Cooke [sic] excelled all others in painting flowers and fruit in the soft delicate manner of old Sèvres, and his imitations are probably to say the least, equal to anything ever turned out of the original factory"—praise indeed! As in Randall's case Cook did not normally sign his factory work although plaques (probably painted in his spare time) and later pieces sometimes carry his signature. He died in 1876.

The figure subjects on the wares in the Sèvres style were painted by James Rouse (b. 1802, d. 1888). Rouse had been trained as a floral artist at the Derby porcelain factory, but during his period at Coalport, from 1830 to 1865, he turned his hand to many subjects which included figures, cupids, pastoral subjects and fruit and floral work. On his own admission he also decorated Coalport porcelain in the Nantgarw manner. Rouse's work on Coalport porcelain was included in the 1851 and 1862 exhibitions. During the 1860's he left Coalport and was employed for a short time at the Cauldon Place Works at Hanley in the Potteries. In 1875 he returned to his native Derby where he worked until his death in 1888 (see Chapter 4).

The Coalport works employed the services of a delicate figure painter, Robert Frederick Abraham (b. 1827, d. 1895) from about 1860. His work was included in the 1862 exhibition (Plate 9). An *Art Journal* writer in that year remarked: "The principal painter of the present day, though there are several other excellent ones, is Mr. Abraham, a student of Antwerp and Paris, and a successful follower of the school of Etty. The softness of touch, the purity and delicacy of feeling, and the sunny mellowness of tone, as well as the chasteness of design and correctness of drawing, produced on the best pieces of this gentleman's productions, show him to be a thorough artist, and place him high above most others in this difficult art." Contrary to the opinion of some writers, R. F. Abraham was only with Coalport for a short time; by 1866 he was Art Director at the Hill Pottery, Burslem, and was described in that year as "the first 'Cupid' painter in the profession" (*Art Journal*, 1866). Subsequently Abraham was Art Director at Copelands, a post he held for thirty years.

In 1862, when W. F. Rose retired, his partner William Pugh became sole proprietor and continued the Coalport traditions on the established lines. At the 1871 Exhibition, as in 1851, the whole emphasis of the Coalport work was on the imitation of continental eighteenth-century styles, and by this time, such work was not only lacking in originality but was also becoming a little outmoded. Among the artists mentioned by name in the periodicals of this period and not already noted were J. Hartshorne (sometimes spelt without the "e") who was a fine cattle and landscape painter and Charles Palmere who was known for his figure subjects and portrait panels.

The Coalport parian, though not produced on such a large scale as at Copelands and Mintons, was nevertheless of fine quality and often shows great technical skill. Ornate figure-supported centrepieces and comports were a special feature.

Unlike many other English potteries, the Coalport works restricted their output to porcelain and there was no production of earthenware or stoneware. William Pugh died in 1875, and after a five-year interval in which a Receiver was appointed and an accumulation of stock cleared, Peter Bruff, an engineer with no previous experience of the industry, acquired the works. In 1889 Peter Bruff was succeeded by his son Charles Bruff. Charles Bruff engaged Thomas John Bott as Art Director in 1890, an engagement that has confused many writers who have mistaken Thomas John for his more famous father Thomas Bott of Worcester (see Chapter 6). Thomas John Bott was born in 1854 and was trained by his father up to the time of the latter's death in 1870. Thomas John Bott had painted for both the Worcester and Brown-Westhead, Moore firms before joining Coalport in 1890; and he continued his connection with the Coalport Company well into the twentieth century, in fact, to the time of his death in 1932. As Art Director he trained many of the later Coalport artists.

Returning to the Victorian artists, mention must be made of Jabez Aston—a floral artist employed over a long period and chiefly known for some signed plaques, often of large size, which are delicately painted with floral studies. W. Birbeck was employed as a landscape artist during the second half of the nineteenth century and later, about 1885, joined Copelands. J. H. Plant was a landscape artist from about 1880 to about 1890 and subsequently joined Doulton's staff at Burslem. Arthur Bowdler was a floral artist practising from about 1875 onwards. The following artists worked mainly in the twentieth century—E. (Ted) O. Ball, J. Beard, F. H. Chivers, F. Howard, Arthur Perry and Percy and Thomas Simpson.

During the closing years of the nineteenth century the Coalport artists were at last allowed to sign their work. These later wares were often "crazed" with a network of fine cracks in the glaze, a defect which does not occur on the earlier Victorian pieces. An important feature of the later wares was the introduction of jewelled enrichments, which consist of small raised blobs of coloured enamel. "This ornamentation is exceedingly rich, and is shown on a great variety of fancy shapes. For the most part these are quite new models, and some of the tall handled vases are true artistic productions. The imitations of jewelled setting is very perfect, particularly the topaz and pearl. Some of the larger pieces—vases . . . have finely painted landscapes and other views on the side" (*Pottery Gazette*, 1892). It may be noticed, however, that the use of jewelling was not new. It was an eighteenth-century technique and had been much used on the more ornate nineteenth-century pieces.

In 1893 the Coalport wares gained a gold medal and considerable publicity at the Chicago World Fair. The late Coalport wares were, however, mostly conservative in following the styles for which the factory had already a reputation. Innovations such as *pâte-sur-pâte* decoration and the "Japanese" style were not attempted. Of the every-day Coalport productions the best known was probably their Indian Tree pattern which had originated about 1801, and it is significant that in the latter part of the century a whole department of decorators was employed at the factory on the production of this pattern.

COALPORT CERAMIC ARTISTS
(*Victorian Period only*)

* Artist given fuller mention in the text.

ABLOTT, RICHARD. Landscape artist from Derby, also worked for Davenports.

*Abraham, Robert Frederick. *c*. 1850–65. Later Art Director, Copelands.
*Aston, Jabez. Floral artist, *c*. 1837–80.
Ball, E. O. (Ted). Landscape artist. Late nineteenth and early twentieth century.
Beard, J. Late nineteenth, early twentieth century.
Birbeck, Joseph. Floral, bird, fruit and fish painter, *c*. 1830–80 (brother to William).
Birbeck, William. Landscape artist, *c*. 1850–80. Later at Copelands.
*Bott, Thomas John. Art Director 1890–1932. See also Brown-Westhead, Moore and Worcester.
Bowdler, Arthur. Floral artist, snowscapes, etc., *c*. 1875–1905.
*Cook, William. Born *c*. 1800. Floral artist, mid-nineteenth century, d. 1876.
Dixon, Thomas. Floral artist, *c*. 1830–70.
Eaton, R. Floral artist, *c*. 1860–85 (also Davenports).
Hall, Arnold. Landscape artist, *c*. 1860–75.
Harper, John. Landscapes.
Hartshorn, J. See Hartshorne, J.
Hartshorne, J. Figure and animal painter, *c*. 1860–80.
Howard, F. Flowers, birds and fruit. Mainly twentieth century.
Jones, Cecil. Floral artist, etc. Mid-nineteeth century.
Keeling, Thomas. Figure painter. Early twentieth century. Also Copelands.
Kelshall. Fruit and floral artist. Mid-nineteenth century.
Latham, John. Floral artist, *c*. 1830–40. An artist of this name was later employed at Mintons.
Lawrence, Stephen. Floral modeller (?), *c*. 1840–70.
Lucas, Daniel, Junior. Scenic artist from Derby, *c*. 1830–50. Later at Copelands.
Mason. Fruit and floral artist. Second half nineteenth century.
Mottershead. Bird painter, *c*. 1830–45.
Mountford, Jesse. Scenic artist from Derby, *c*. 1821–40. Later at Davenports.
Palmere, Charles. Figure subjects, heads, etc. Mid-nineteenth century. Also Worcester.
Parker, John. Floral and bird painter.
Pattern, Josiah. Crests and wild flowers.

PERRY, ARTHUR, H. Landscapes, birds, fish, etc. Mainly twentieth century. Also Copelands and Doultons.

PLANT, J. H. Landscape and animal subjects, c. 1880–90. Later at Wedgwoods and Doultons.

*RANDALL, JOHN. Born 1810. Bird painter of repute, c. 1835–81, d. 1910.

*ROUSE, JAMES. Born 1802. Floral and figure artist, c. 1830–65. Also Derby.

SIMPSON, PERCY. Landscapes, game birds, etc. twentieth century. Retired 1956.

SIMPSON, THOMAS. Father of Percy. Foreman painter. Late nineteenth, early twentieth century.

STEELE, THOMAS, JUNIOR. Landscape painter trained at Derby, c. 1845–50, d. c. 1850.

STEPHENS, HAMLET. Sèvres-type floral patterns. Mid-nineteenth century.

TREVIES, WILLIAM. Floral artist.

WILLIAMS, JOHN. Floral and bird painter.

WORRELL. Modeller. Mid-nineteenth century.

COALPORT MARKS

Mark No.

1 Pre-Victorian mark, c. 1820.

2 Mark occurring on service made for Queen Victoria, c. 1837.

COALPORT 45

Mark No.

3   Various marks incorporating the title John (or J) Rose & Co., 1825–50.

4   Copies of Sèvres, Dresden and Chelsea marks were used c. 1845–55.

5   "C.B.D." (Coalbrookdale) mark used c. 1851–61.

6   C.S.N. (Caughley, Swansea, Nantgarw) "ampersand" mark used c. 1861–75.

7   c. 1875–81.

8   Crowned Coalport mark, c. 1881–91.

9   "England" added c. 1891. Impressed potting date marks occur on some late pieces, e.g. "12 K 01" for 1901.

COALPORT PATTERN NUMBERS

The early wares do not generally bear pattern numbers, nor do the mid-nineteenth-century copies of Sèvres and Chelsea porcelain, or the individual examples painted by leading artists.

Late COALPORT pattern numbers were prefixed by various letters, each denoting a special class.

       V for vases.
       X and Z for dinner and dessert wares.
       Y for tea wares.

Vases and other objects may also bear size and model numbers, i.e. S/S 156 (small size), M/S156 (middle size), L/S156 (large size).

The model prefixes Toy, Min, 1st, 2nd, 3rd and 4th relate to sizes and are self-explanatory.

The pattern number reached by 1900 was in the region of 5000.

COALPORT DESSERT PLATE.   1851 EXHIBITION

CHAPTER 3

COPELAND & GARRETT
and COPELAND

JOSIAH SPODE, the founder of the factory that bore his name, died in 1797 and was succeeded by his son Josiah Spode II (1754-1827), who began making porcelain about 1795, introducing the famed English bone china body. Spode III succeeded his father in 1827 but died two years later, and in 1833 the business was bought from the executors by William Taylor Copeland, a former partner of the Spodes, who took into partnership Thomas Garrett, the firm's principal salesman. The Copeland & Garrett partnership lasted from 1833 to 1847 and it was during this period that the parian body was introduced and developed (see Chapter 7).

The *Art Union* magazine of 1846 includes an interesting article, one of a series entitled "Illustrated Tour in the Manufacturing Districts", giving an account of the Copeland & Garrett factory and productions. The following two paragraphs incorporate salient points included in this contemporary review.

The Copeland & Garrett works extended over nearly eleven acres and gave employment to about one thousand people. Particular emphasis is placed on the large assortment of slabs, for fireplaces (Plate 13), table tops, finger plates and general door furniture, all of which afforded opportunities for the artists to display their skill. Slabs forty-six inches by twenty-four inches are mentioned as being made for dressing tables and washstands. An interesting note is included giving 1825 as the first date for the introduction of these large panels: the early examples were, however, ". . . very humble specimens indeed, as compared with those since produced. . . ."

Attention is also drawn to the widespread use of "Etruscan" or classical, shapes and patterns. Several articles intended for garden and conservatory use are listed; these include garden seats, vases for orange trees, flower boxes and pillars—"many of which are of very large dimensions, and of very great excellence. . . ." Copeland & Garrett's statuary porcelain, or parian, is naturally mentioned, as are dessert, tea and dinner services—"breakfast services, toilet services and hundreds of other important objects, sold 'in masses', and exported in 'crates' by the thousand. . . . Unsurpassed in Great Britain in excellence of material, form and ornamentation. . . ."

The engraving reproduced on page 21 shows typical productions of this period.

Little is known of Copeland & Garrett's ceramic artists. The Art Director was Thomas Battam (b. 1810, d. 1864) and to him must be given much of the credit for the quality of the firm's productions during this period. Thomas Battam came of a family of ceramic artists and received his early training at his father's decorating establishment in Gough Square, London. The classical shapes and "Etruscan" patterns seen on many Copeland & Garrett useful wares were due to his influence. It is probable that Battam also painted some of the large "slabs" which received such praise in contemporary notices. The *Pottery Gazette* of 1882 contains the following reference to his work: "The late Mr. Battam, Art Superintendent at Messrs. Copelands, did some magnificent works for the Sutherland family, on large china slabs, prepared for the purpose, he copied a few of the oil paintings at Trentham Hall and gave every satisfaction in his elaborate work, receiving from two hundred to three hundred guineas for a single enamel painting." Battam also played an important part in developing the parian body. He was the founder and President of the Crystal Palace Art Union (founded in 1858), and had himself a fine collection of Victorian ceramics which was sold at Christies in 1865. He had left Copelands' employment by 1856 and was then living in London.

The firm's flower paintings were discussed in the *Art Union* of 1846: ". . . some of the flower pieces on Copeland and Garrett's stall are painted in very subdued tones, and have not only the natural appearance of flowers seen behind sunshine, but have the suggestive force of calling imagination into action to explain the atmosphere haze, which actually reveals, while it seems to hide, the beauty of the floral group". These were the work of a former Swansea artist, David Evans, whose name is not usually associated with Copeland & Garrett's porcelain. A typical example of his work now in the Victoria & Albert Museum is illustrated here (Plate 12).

David Evans was born about 1795. He is recorded as a painter of wild flowers at the Swansea porcelain factory from about 1814 to 1826, and he was afterwards employed at Worcester (the Grainger factory), Coalport, Mintons, Copelands and at the Alcock factory.

The *Pottery Gazette* of 1881 refers to Evans as "the late David Evans—one of the finest wild flower painters in the world". Subsequently, it is observed that "David Evans was not excelled as a wild flower painter. It was a remark in the trade that you might blow his wild roses off the ware, they appeared so light and real." It is recorded (*Pottery Gazette*, 1883) that he painted the most elaborate china chimney pieces and tables for the houses of the nobility and these would doubtless have been produced during his term with Copeland & Garrett who specialised in such productions.

David Evans's son, William, has left an interesting account of his father's methods: ". . . Backgrounds are sometimes used in the dust form, but are always finished with the finest work of the camel-hair pencil, the painting undergoing more than one or two fires. . . . David Evans used to give the last touches to the hearts and edges of his flowers with the purest white enamel, like seed pearls, and streaks of light. . . . The pencil used by Evans in this work was a fine, small camel-hair one. . . . Mr. Evans would use only the colours of certain makers and these colours he would travel miles to obtain" (*Pottery Gazette*, 1887).

The Copeland & Garrett partnership came to an end in the summer of 1847. On the retirement of Thomas Garrett, W. T. Copeland used the title "W. T. Copeland, late Spode" until 1867 when he took his four sons into partnership and the name of the firm then became W. T. Copeland and Sons.

The Copeland porcelain included in the 1851 Exhibition has been reviewed in Chapter 1. Throughout the third quarter of the century the Copeland parian, or "statuary porcelain" as it was known at Copelands, was being commented upon and praised in reviews of ceramic work. "Alderman Copeland has devoted so much attention to his Statuary Porcelain, and he has produced these works in such numbers, variety and beauty, that he may justly claim to be considered to stand at the head of this department of Art Manufacture" (*Art Journal*, 1859). The Copeland porcelain dessert services often had elaborate comports supported by parian figures (see Chapter 7).

David Evans was succeeded as Copelands' foremost floral artist by Charles Ferdinand Hürten. While Evans mainly confined himself to small-scale painting, Hürten was at his best in large powerful studies. C. F. Hürten, as he normally signed himself, was born in Cologne in 1818. While in his late teens he went to Paris, where he painted floral designs for various decorating establishments and also carried out special commissions for the Sèvres factory. It was his forceful paintings included in the 1858 Paris Exhibition that brought him to the notice of Copelands, who engaged him in 1859. He remained with them until ill health forced him to retire in 1897. Hürten's studies were taken direct from nature or from spirited gouache drawings which he had previously taken from nature. An *Art Journal* reporter in 1874 observed that Hürten "has no superior in flower painting, especially on pieces sufficiently large to give full scope to his vigorous yet delicate pencil; and his perfect feeling for all the beauties of texture and colour in his favourite subjects is sufficiently obvious. He makes us see he is as much a florist as an artist, and as true a student of form as of colour." Other contemporary reports also speak in glowing terms, such as a writer in the *Pottery Gazette* trade journal of May 1893, who remarked that C. F. Hürten "has attained and deservedly so, the distinction of being one of, if not the first, flower painter in Europe". The examples shown in Plates 18 and 20 may be regarded as typical of his work.

A speciality of the firm was their jewelled ware, the technical excellence of which is probably greater than its artistic merit. Apart from the floral painting for which Copelands were well known, the scenic painting on decorative vases and on dessert ware was mostly from the hand of Daniel Lucas, Junr. His work was included in the 1862 London Exhibition: "Mr. Copeland's landscape subjects were also exceedingly good. The scenes after Turner, the Ancient Italy vase etc. painted by Lucas, were all of very great merit, delicately painted, and excellently gilded" (*Waring's Masterpieces*). Plate 17 is an example of Lucas's painting after Turner. Daniel Lucas, Junr. was the youngest son of the Derby scenic artist of the same name and was himself apprenticed at Derby. On leaving Copelands' employment about 1870 he set up a small decorating workshop where he painted wares for other manufacturers. He was succeeded at Copelands by W. Birbeck.

George Eyre (b. 1818, d. 1887) succeeded Thomas Battam, as Art Director. He had previously been employed at Mintons, Alcocks and the latter's successors Sir James Duke & Nephews, for whom he decorated wares included in the 1862 Exhibition. George Eyre is also known for his spirited figure painting on various earthenware bodies. He was soon succeeded by Robert Frederick Abraham, the former Coalport figure painter whose work has been discussed already in Chapter 2. Abraham served as Art Director at Copelands until his death in 1895.

In the 1870's Copelands were fortunate to have the services of a figure painter, Lucien Besche, who had trained in France and had been, for a brief period, with Mintons. The *Art Journal* review of the 1873 Vienna Exhibition commended some Copeland vases decorated with Watteau figure subjects by this artist. The vase illustrated in Plate 19, painted with a continuous panel of children, may be regarded as a typical specimen of his signed work. Besche's period of ceramic painting was comparatively short. In 1885 he forsook his career as a ceramic painter and moved to London where he painted in oils, designed costumes and drew illustrations for magazines. He died in 1901.

Copelands did not, to any great extent, attempt to copy the Sèvres forms and motifs so popular at the Coalport factory and at Mintons. They did however follow the lead given by Worcester in Japanese styles during the 1870's and 1880's and, as at Worcester, these examples were finely finished especially in the matt and tooled gilding. The Copeland gilding, often chased, was always of good quality and was used with restraint. Copelands made hundreds of thousands of parian figures, but their production of ordinary porcelain figures was practically non-existent; and this is true of the later Victorian manufacturers in general, with the exception of the Royal Worcester works.

Of the later Copeland ceramic artists, mention must be made of Robert John Abraham, the son of the Art Director, R. F. Abraham. R. J. Abraham was trained at the Stoke School of Art and at South Kensington where he won a gold medal in 1872. Another artist of some significance was John Arrowsmith, who was at first a floral artist but turned his attention mainly to bird painting in the twentieth century.

Samuel Alcock, an unusually fine figure painter, received his training at the Royal Academy schools and was employed by Copelands from the 1880's into the twentieth century. Examples of his work are illustrated in Plates 21 and 23. His painting is soft and delicate and in the manner of L. Alma-Tadema. He made good use of the uncoloured porcelain body to set off a figure composition to the greatest effect, and he was one of the few Victorian ceramic artists to depict figures in contemporary dress

(Plate 23) although much of his work is classical in style. Alcock's work is always associated with fine gilt or jewelled borders and enrichments.

The *Art Journal* of 1896 refers to Alcock as being "the principal artist of the establishment". Another contemporary account printed in the firm's handbook concerns the visit of the Princess of Wales to the Copeland works in 1897: ". . . among the extensive display of articles was a stand of the charming pieces decorated in Mr. Alcock's peculiarly delicate style upon the glossiest of surfaces. The Cavendish vase, which formed the centre of the collection, is a magnificent specimen, decorated on the body with groups of classical figures representing 'Night' and 'Morning', the top, foot and handles of the piece being gorgeously gilt and 'jewelled'. Dainty dessert pieces, painted with sylvan subjects and vases decorated with subjects representing the seasons, music and the arts were also on view." As might be expected, Alcock normally signed his work.

Charles Brough painted floral, bird, fish and figure subjects at Copelands before joining Doultons' staff in 1903. In 1897, on the occasion of a visit by the Prince of Wales, the firm's handbook states that he "was engaged upon a copy of the Windsor vase, now in the possession of the Queen, an elegant ornament, typical of the artistic reproductions of the firm in porcelain". James Weaver was a bird painter who was working at Copelands for a long period. The *Pottery Gazette* of 1892 contains a reference to "the two Weavers, father and son, such fine bird painters". Charles Weaver the son painted mainly cattle subjects but retired early in life owing to ill health. Some forceful scenic painting, often on porcelain or earthenware plaques, was carried out towards the end of the century by W. Yale (Plate 22).

While emphasis has been laid on the artists responsible for decorating the Copeland products, it must be remembered that the porcelain and glaze itself, was also of excellent quality. The glaze is remarkably free from crazing, that troublesome net-work of hair-like cracks that is the bane of so much, otherwise perfect, porcelain. The delicate ground colours are even and constant, while the quality of the gold and jewelled enrichments has already been remarked upon.

Although this volume is concerned primarily with Victorian porcelain, mention must be made of some of the other wares produced by Copelands. Llewelyn Jewitt, writing in 1878 (*The Ceramic*

Art of Great Britain), is high in his praise of the Copeland Ivory body: "... nothing could be less grating to the eye of taste than this soft tint, and doubtless in many homes of taste, the warm 'ivory body' will take the place of the cold white of the general classes of earthenware". Many spirited models of animals and garden vases were produced in colourful "Majolica" ware.

One of the Copeland specialities was the production of painted tiles, mostly earthenware, for interior decoration. Apart from the normal day-to-day patterns and commissions, momentous undertakings in this field are recorded. One, the ceiling to the Imperial Library in Paris, consisted of nine cupolas, each comprising 4000 curved tiles.

COPELAND ARTISTS

* Artist given fuller mention in the text

*ABRAHAM, ROBERT FREDERICK. Art Director 1865–95 (also Coalport).

*ABRAHAM, ROBERT JOHN. Born 1850, employed *c.* 1875, d. *c.* 1925.

ADAMS, F. W. Floral and fruit painter. Late nineteenth and early twentieth century.

*ALCOCK, SAMUEL. Born *c.* 1846. Figure painter from *c.* 1880 into twentieth century.

ARROWSMITH, JOHN. Bird and floral subjects. Late nineteenth and early twentieth century.

BALL, T. (?). *c.* 1870–90.

BANCROFT, JOSEPH. Floral artist from Derby, *c.* 1830–40. Later at Mintons.

BATTAM, FREDERICK. Designer, etc., *c.* 1870.

*BATTAM, THOMAS. Born 1810. Art Director from *c.* 1835–57, d. 1864.

*BESCHE, LUCIEN. From France, employed *c.* 1872–85. Also Mintons, d. 1901.

BIRBECK, WILLIAM. *c.* 1885. Landscape artist from Coalport, *c.* 1887.

BOURNE. Floral and fruit painter. Mid-nineteenth century.

BRAYFORD. *c.* 1880+.

*BROUGH, CHARLES B. Floral, game bird subjects, etc. Late nineteenth century. Joined Doultons *c.* 1903.

CARTLIDGE, JOHN. Floral artist. Mid-nineteenth century.

DEAN, J. Floral artist, c. 1880–90.

*EVANS, DAVID. Floral artist, c. 1840–55. Also Worcester, Alcocks etc.

*EYRE, GEORGE. Born 1818. Art Director, c. 1864–65, d. 1887.

EYRE, JOHN. Born 1847. Designer, c. 1874–80. Also Doultons, (Lambeth), d. 1927.

HALSE. Modeller. Mid-nineteenth century.

HASSALL, THOMAS. Born 1878. Ceramic painter from 1892. Art Director from 1910, d. 1940.

*HÜRTEN, C. F. Born 1818. Floral artist. Employed 1859–97, d. 1901.

LEE, HARRY. Floral and bird painter. Late nineteenth century.

*LUCAS, DANIEL, JUNR. Scenic painter, apprenticed at Derby, worked c. 1850–70.

MELI, G. Sculptor and modeller, c. 1840–50.

MICKLEWRIGHT. Landscape painter. Late nineteenth century.

MOUNTFORD, JOHN. Figure modeller from Derby. Discovered parian body c. 1844. Later worked for Mintons and on his own.

PERRY, ARTHUR. Born 1871. Scenic, bird painter, etc., c. 1899 and c. 1907–25. Also Coalport and Doultons.

SADLER, T. Floral artist. Late nineteenth century.

SALT. Designer. Late nineteenth century.

SMITH, J. Floral artist, c. 1865 (from Mintons).

WALLACE, R. Gilder and jeweller. Late nineteenth century.

WEAVER, JAMES. Bird subjects (from Worcester). Second half nineteenth century, d. c. 1880.

WEAVER, CHARLES. Cattle, bird subjects, etc. Late nineteenth century.

*YALE, W. Scenic artist. Late nineteenth century. Worked on his own account after leaving Copelands.

12. COPELAND AND GARRETT plate, probably painted by David Evans. *c.* 1840. Mark No. 11. *Victoria & Albert Museum.*

13
COPELAND AND GARRETT fireplace panels richly decorated on a lavender ground. *c.* 1845. 39½ in. × 10 in. Mark No. 11.

14
COPELAND AND GARRETT model of a greyhound, one of a pair—typical of several animal models. *c.* 1845. 11 in. × 4 in. Mark No. 11.

15. COPELAND vase and cover decorated in the Sèvres manner. 1851 Exhibition. Ht. 11¾ in. *Victoria & Albert Museum.*

16
COPELAND ewer, the scenic panel painted by Daniel Lucas, Junr. 1851 Exhibition. Ht. 15¼ in. Mark No. 16A. *Victoria & Albert Museum.*

17
COPELAND vase, the panel painted by Daniel Lucas, Junr. after J. M. W. Turner's 'Phryne going to the Public Baths as Venus'. *c.* 1862. Ht. 23½ in. Mark 'Copeland' printed and impressed.

Page 58

18

Top Left: COPELAND vase, the panel painted by C. F. Hurten. *c.* 1870. Ht. 28 in. Mark No. 16B. *Copeland Works Museum.*

19

Top Right: COPELAND vase with pierced cover, the body painted with a continuous panel of dancing children. Signed L. Besche. *c.* 1880. Ht. 15 in. Mark No. 16B.

20

Left. COPELAND earthenware plaque painted by C. F. Hurten. *c.* 1875. 24 in. × 18 in.

Page 59

21. COPELAND vase, the continuous band of figures painted by S. Alcock. *c.* 1890. Ht. 31 in. *Copeland Works Museum.*

22
COPELAND plaque, painted by the scenic artist W. Yale. *c.* 1885. 17½ in × 12 in.

23
COPELAND 'Jewelled Porcelain' plate painted by S. Alcock inscribed 'Court Costume 1895'. *c.* 1895. (impressed date cypher). Mark No. 20

24. DERBY plaque painted by John Haslem, marked with the Dresden crossed swords mark. *c.* 1830–40. 9⅛ in. × 7 in. *Victoria & Albert Museum.*

25
DERBY plaque decorated with rich blue border and chased gold enrichments. Painted in the Sèvres style and bearing a mock Sèvres mark. c. 1840. 5 in. × 4 in. Mark No. 25.

26
Pair of unglazed STEVENSON & HANCOCK figures, taken from 18th century Derby factory moulds. c. 1865. Ht. 6¾ in. Mark No. 27 (incised).

Page 63

27
Group of CROWN
DERBY Japan patterns.
c. 1885–90.

28
CROWN DERBY covered
vase (one of a pair)
decorated with birds
and floral motifs on a
yellow ground.
c. 1880. Ht. 16½ in.
Mark No. 28.

COPELAND & GARRETT AND COPELAND MARKS

Mark No.

10 All marks bearing the name "Spode" without additions are pre-Victorian.

11 "Copeland & Garrett" in various forms used from 1833 to 1847.

12 1833–47.

13 Rare Copeland & Garrett mark printed in gold, 1833–47.

COPELAND, LATE SPODE.

14 Printed or impressed, 1847–67.

Mark No.	
15	Printed mark, 1847–67.
16a	Simple form of crossed C's was used c. 1847–56.
16b	Ornate version, c. 1867–85. The single word "Copeland" sometimes occurs, printed or impressed.
17	Printed mark, c. 1875–90.
18	Small impressed date marks occur showing the month and year in which the piece was potted. F 88 = February 1888.
19	Late nineteenth-century printed mark, from c. 1894. (The date figure was impressed in the body at this period.)
20	Late nineteenth-century mark, used into twentieth century. "England" added to marks, c. 1891.

COPELAND 67

COPELAND & GARRETT AND COPELAND PATTERN NUMBERS

A simple progressive system of pattern numbering employed during the earlier part of the century was continued into the Copeland & Garrett period (1833-47). Pattern numbers ranging from about 4500 to 7200 were brought into use at this period. The system was continued by the Copeland Company from 1847 until 9999 was reached in about 1852. From this time a new series bearing the prefix D was used which ran up to D.9999 in the late 1870's.

At the termination of the D numbers a division was made, the porcelain patterns being prefixed 1/, the earthenware 2/. The number for porcelain patterns had reached 1/9929 by January 1900, and shortly afterwards a new prefix "R" was adopted.

'UTILITARIAN OBJECTS' 1846

CHAPTER 4

DERBY

THE town of Derby will always rank high in the history of ceramics on account of the fine porcelain made there under the two William Duesburys in the eighteenth century. The period in which we are interested here dates back to 1811 when Robert Bloor, formerly a clerk and salesman at the factory, took over the factory. To enable him to pay the instalments of the agreed purchase price Bloor was compelled to lower the standards of workmanship and to concentrate on gaudy "Japan" patterns with their large areas of red, blue and gold—work which could be produced quickly and cheaply by semi-skilled hands. Furthermore Bloor finished and sold great quantities of "seconds" or slightly imperfect ware with which he flooded the markets. Although he was successful in paying off his debt his policy resulted in the downfall of the factory.

Porcelain of the Bloor period is often disfigured by a badly crazed glaze through the minute cracks of which liquids can soak and stain the body. The overglaze enamel colours tended to be rather thick and to flake away from the glaze leaving unsightly white spots. Despite this, many good ceramic artists were employed at the factory, and among these mention must be made of William Dexter, John Haslem, Daniel Lucas, James Rouse, William Slater, Edwin Steele, Horatio Steele, Thomas Steele, Senr. and Thomas Steele, Junr. Other artists such as Joseph Bancroft, William Corden, William Dixon, Richard Dodson, Jesse Mountford and Moses Webster had left Derby by 1830, mostly as a result of Bloor's policy of austerity.

Of the artists who remained and who decorated Derby porcelain during the opening years of the Victorian era, John Haslem is of particular interest. Any student of Derby porcelain must be deeply indebted to this artist for the useful account of the factory and its workpeople which he wrote under the title *The Old Derby China Factory*. John Haslem was born in 1808 and, at the age of fourteen, he was apprenticed to the Derby factory. At first he specialised in floral work but later turned to figure painting, a subject in which he proved so skilful that he was able to take the place of William Corden as chief figure artist when Corden left the factory about 1820. Haslem painted a number of china plaques with Watteau and other figure subjects in the style of Dresden and Sèvres, and these often bore forged marks. These imitations of continental wares always have richly tooled gold borders in keeping with their style. Haslem relates that he and Corden were in the habit of partially washing over the space reserved for the delicate flesh colours with a thin coating of soft white enamel and in this manner obtained a pleasing texture.

Haslem moved to London, where he carried out many fine paintings on porcelain as well as some fine enamels on metal. From 1844 to 1851 he was employed by Queen Victoria in copying family portraits and Old Masters at Windsor Castle, Osborne House and Buckingham Palace. In 1857 he returned to Derby, but by this time the original factory had closed. He died in 1884.

Daniel Lucas, Senr., the Derby scenic painter, was born in 1788. He was trained at the Davenport works and joined the Derby factory in the early 1830's, remaining there until its closure in 1848. Although Haslem states that Lucas "was the principal landscape painter employed at Derby" and that "his work, therefore, is probably oftener met with than that of any other of the Derby landscape painters", the identification of his work has so far been little more than intelligent guesswork based on the general impression that his style can be compared with that of a painter in oils— a branch of the art which he did indeed practise. When considering the identification of the work of any of the Derby artists of this period it must be remembered that none of these was permitted to sign his work. Daniel Lucas, who had three sons all apprenticed at Derby, died in Birmingham about 1867.

William Slater was a painter of fruit, insects and armorial motifs who also excelled in chased gold enrichments. He had originally been apprenticed at the small porcelain factory at Pinxton changing his allegiance to Derby in 1813. When the Derby factory closed Slater was employed at Davenports of Longport up to the time of his death, at the age of seventy-three, in 1867. Several of his sons were later known for their work in various fields of ceramic decoration.

Among the many artists connected with Derby porcelain Thomas Steele was outstanding. His most famous and prized work consists of highly finished porcelain plaques painted with fruit and flowers. Haslem enlarges on the work of this artist in the following manner:

"Thomas Steele, whose fruit painting on china has never been surpassed was a native of the Staffordshire Potteries, where he first learned his art. He worked at the Derby factory from 1815. . . . Steele painted both flowers and insects well, but as a painter of fruit on china he had no superior if, indeed, he had any equal in his day. His colour is remarkably pleasing, being rich and transparent, and his large fruit pieces are painted with great force. His grouping is harmonious, the light and shade well managed, each piece of fruit is well rounded, and the outlines softened and blended into the one next it, each partaking of the reflected colour from the other, a matter not always attended to by either china or other painters. Many of Steele's effects were cleverly produced by carefully dabbing on the colour, while wet, with his finger, thus blending the various tints well into each other, and giving great softness and delicacy with an appearance of high finish, as if by elaborate stippling." After leaving Derby about 1825 he was employed by Davenports and then by Mintons. He died in 1850.

Three of Steele's sons were apprentices at Derby. Edwin painted flowers and, like his father, was subsequently employed at Mintons. Horatio painted a Derby dessert service for Queen Victoria about 1842. The youngest son, Thomas, was a landscape painter who died at an early age while employed at the Coalport factory.

Of the many modellers employed at Derby early in the nineteenth century, Cocker is of particular interest to the student of Victorian ceramics. George Cocker (b. 1794, d. 1868) was apprenticed at the factory about 1808 and was employed there as a modeller until 1826, except for a break from 1817 to 1821 when he worked at Coalport and Worcester. In 1826 he left the factory and with a fellow worker, John Whittaker Senr., established a small factory in Friar Gate, Derby. An early notice of this venture reads: "Ladies or Gentlemen may have figures, ornaments etc. executed from models or drawings of their own" and "a variety of Tea and Dessert services of modern and approved pattern" are also mentioned. George Cocker's name is mainly associated with a range of well modelled figures in a white biscuit body; examples sometimes bear his name or that of his son D. Cocker incised into the body. (Sampson Hancock re-issued many of Cocker's models in the second half of the nineteenth century). In 1878 Llewellyn Jewitt noted: "His figures and busts, of which he produced a goodly variety . . . produced both in biscuit and painted. They were very clever and meritorious. He also made, rather extensively, as they met a ready sale, small baskets of beautifully formed raised flowers, and brooches and other trinkets in the same way ... groups of animals were also produced." Cocker later worked in London and in the Potteries, notably for Mintons.

In 1828 Bloor's health failed, and the factory was managed by James Thomason until 1844 when Thomas Clarke took control. The original Derby factory was finally closed in 1848 and many of the old Derby moulds and factory furnishings were sold in the Potteries. However, some of the former workmen banded together under William Locker and, making use of old models and using established patterns, inaugurated and worked a small factory in King Street, Derby, where they continued the Derby tradition. The products of this period were, until Locker's death in 1859, occasionally marked "Locker & Co. Late Bloor". Subsequent marks that occur on later wares are "Stevenson & Co.", "Stevenson, Sharp & Co." and "Stevenson & Hancock", but in many cases the wares were marked with the old Crown Derby crossed baton mark. In 1862 following a suggestion by the ceramic historian Llewellyn Jewitt, the initials S.H. were added, one either side of this old mark (No. 27). On the death of Stevenson, Sampson Hancock, the sole survivor of the original band of craftsmen, took over the management, a position that he kept up to the time of his death in 1898.

The initials "S.H." fitted both Stevenson & Hancock and Sampson Hancock and this mark was retained by the latter. It is interesting to notice that this factory, which styled itself "The Old Crown Derby China Works", continued in production at King Street, Derby, well into the twentieth century.

Of the products of the King Street factory Haslem, writing in 1876, states: "For a number of years after its commencement, a good deal of ware was turned out in the style of the later Old Derby patterns, and a great deal of matching was, from time to time, done, the most important being, on several occasions, the making up of losses by breakage of the dessert service made for Her Majesty in 1842. This was done in a manner to give perfect satisfaction. Many of the old Derby figures have also been made, particularly a set of the four Seasons, and some have, at sales of old Derby China, realised considerable prices, under the impression that they were genuine 'old Derby'. Of late years attention has been specially directed to the making of a larger class of figures, and more particularly of ornamental ware in which modelled flowers have been a chief feature. In the latter style numerous frames for looking glasses have been made of superior quality. . . ."

Later wares include fine dessert services and specimen plates hand painted with delicate floral compositions, birds and local scenery, floral encrusted vases and baskets and figures and groups after early Derby originals. Many colourful "Japan" patterns were also produced in red, blue and gold, and pieces bearing these traditional patterns (the factory terms being "Old Crown Derby Witches", "Old Crown Derby Rose", "Old Crown Derby Garden" etc.) include pastille burners, bottle vases, covered boxes, small trays, miniature watering cans and other objects, and coffee and bridge services mounted in fitted cases.

A *Pottery Gazette* writer in 1895 states that Hancock ". . . employed from time to time some of the best modern china painters, and some of his productions in the Japanese style are marvels of beauty and colouring". Of the artists employed at King Street mention must be made of James Rouse of whom Hancock himself remarked: "In 1875 I engaged Mr. James Rouse—to me for the ensuing seven years he proved a valuable workman, for, being so good a general hand, he was able to paint all kinds of subjects that were required" (*Pottery Gazette*, 1895). James Rouse was born in Derby in 1802. He was apprenticed to the old Crown Derby factory where he had the good fortune to work under the guidance of the famous William (Quaker) Pegg. While in his early twenties Rouse left Derby and was employed by John Rose at the Coalport factory. It was while he was employed at Coalport that Rouse turned his hand to subjects other than floral; he painted Coalport porcelain in the Sèvres style with cupid and figure subjects for inclusion in the 1851 and 1862 Exhibitions and painted some portrait miniatures on porcelain. After some thirty years, Rouse left Coalport and worked for a few years at the Cauldon Place factory at Hanley before moving to Birmingham, where he was engaged in painting enamelled jewellery, brooches and studs. In 1875 he returned to his native Derby, and, as we have seen, he was then engaged by Sampson Hancock at the King Street factory for a period of seven years, painting "all kinds of subjects".

Sampson Hancock was succeeded in 1898 by his grandson James Robinson. The twentieth-century proprietors were W. Larcombe and F. Howard Paget. It should be noticed that no printed decoration occurs on King Street wares, and all examples are hand painted.

In 1876 a separate Company was formed under the title of the Derby Crown Porcelain Company, and a large factory was built on a site in Osmaston Road. It seems that there were some initial delays and that the factory did not start production on a commercial scale until 1878. Edward Phillips from the Royal Worcester factory, together with his fellow directors in the new venture, sought from the first to exploit the large American market for fine decorative porcelain. Once again the colourful, traditional Derby "Japan" patterns (Plate 27) were used, but many new vase shapes were modelled and "they are of every conceivable design and style of decoration" (*Pottery Gazette*, 1880). Of the early modellers the following names are recorded in contemporary notices: R. G. Morris, Ingram, Bourne, Stephen and Warrington Hogg "to whose prolific hand many of the modern shapes at Derby owe their origin" (*Pottery Gazette*, 1893).

An account of the new Derby factory and their products in 1884 is contained in Cassell's *Magazine of Art* of that year:

> While the promoters of the revival of the manufacture of Derby china have respected with becoming reverence the artistic tradition of the "old Derby" school, and reproduced its more famous patterns, they have not been content to remain mere plagiarists in porcelain. . . . The plaques are larger than those attempted at the old works, those from the pencil of Mr. Landgraff . . . being paintings of exceptional delicacy of drawing and colouring. The "figures", too, of the new factory are larger than those of the past, and modelling more correct. While the quaint and grotesque patterns, such as Dr. Syntax, the Mansion House Dwarfs, etc., have been revived, something more than mere replication in this direction is aimed at. For instance, there is an original series of statuettes, representing "Tribulation", "Supplication", "Resignation" and "Adoration" with one or two spirited essays in the classic, and certain droll illustrations of "Force" and "Persuasion" in which a monk and a mule are the leading characters. . . . Raised gold work is a favourite form of decoration of the present factory. It combines nearly all the porcelain decorator's method of gaining richness of effect: opulent ground-colour, gold, burnished and dead, gem-like enamelling, and so forth. This raised-gold treatment is applied to dinner and dessert services,

likewise to teaware; but it is displayed with the most lavish advantage in the luxurious fish and game plates, of which wealthy Americans are the largest purchasers. . . . The mere catalogue descriptions, "fish and game plates" conveys no adequate idea of these elaborate pictures in porcelain framed in gold. . . . Prominent are services of raised gold dessert plates enriched with Venetian vignettes, the design of which, I should note, is due to Mr. Richard Lunn, the Art Director of the Company.

Another style of treatment that separates the "old Derby" from the "new" is the rich Persian decoration, which entirely covers the service of the article decorated. Divers schemes of colouring are brought into requisition, and intricate ornament is in raised gold, sometimes jewelled. "Egg-shell" is still another pattern, the delicate fragility of the ware being well described by that designation. "Ivory" ware is a dainty imitation of the material which it assimilates; while "perforated" china, graceful and basket-like, is another happy departure from conventionalism. The Derby works of today have also achieved a creditable triumph in "stained bodies" of delicate mauves and greens. . . . The art directorate of South Kensington has encouraged the Derby factory by ordering reproductions of blue Rhodian and Persian rice dishes, bottles and other objects. . . . Such reproductions have been attempted in Germany and France, but the authorities of South Kensington are best satisfied with the Derby transcripts. Among these replicas for South Kensington may be cited an ambitious vase of Imari ware. . . .

The influential patronage which was extended to the "old Derby" factory has not been wanting at the new works. Wealthy Americans are, perhaps, the largest purchasers of modern Derby. An opulent tourist will pay four or five hundred pounds for his decorated Derby dinner service. . . . But modern Derby china does not appeal to the millionaires of the New World alone, a dainty dinner service has been supplied to the Prince of Wales, and from the Derby "Crown" Porcelain Company came the historical dessert service which working-men of the Liberal party presented to Mr. Gladstone; with landscapes by Count Holtzendorf, the chief artist of the Derby factory. . . . Other Derby artists whose work gives evidence of present capacity and future potentiality are Mr. James Hogg, the modeller, Mr. Platts, Mr. Dickson [sic] and Mr. Keene, the younger.

In October 1882 James Rouse left the King Street factory and joined the new Osmaston Road Company. Here he was chiefly employed on fine floral painting (Plate 29) and although now approaching eighty years of age, his work showed no signs of deterioration. At this period Rouse's work is often signed. He died in February 1888 while engaged in painting the floral panels of a dessert service made for presentation to Mr. Gladstone. His son, Charles Rouse was also employed at the Derby factory as a gilder, and worked on the same Gladstone service.

James Rouse was succeeded by Desiré Leroy from Mintons. Leroy, who painted birds and floral compositions in the French style, is perhaps best known for his delightful paintings in white enamel on a rich dark blue ground (Plate 30). Examples bearing the signatures of A. Gregory (flowers), W. E. J. Dean (scenic and marine subjects), and C. Gresley (landscapes and flowers) belong to the twentieth century.

In January 1890 the Company was appointed "Manufacturers of Porcelain to Her Majesty", and given the privilege of using the title "The Royal Crown Derby Porcelain Company". The use of the title "Royal" in the printed factory mark is therefore a useful guide to dating the later wares (mark No. 29). An earthenware body was sometimes used for the table wares. The factory prospered and in 1895 some five hundred people were employed.

In conclusion it is interesting to look forward into the twentieth century and to see the union of the old eighteenth-century factory with the modern factory. In April 1935, the King Street factory was bought up and amalgamated with the Royal Crown Derby works which thus gained possession of the original Derby patterns and moulds. They also gained the potter's wheel which was reputed to have been used by the first William Duesbury and had been rescued by William Locker when the original factory closed down in 1848.

DERBY CERAMIC ARTISTS
(*Victorian Period only*)

* Artist given fuller mention in the text.

ABLOTT, RICHARD. Landscape artist, *c.* 1845, later worked for Davenports.
BARNET, JAMES. Stevenson & Hancock (King Street), modeller, etc.

BOURNE. Modeller, Royal Crown Derby, *c.* 1885–90.

BROUGHTON, JOSEPH. Bloor period up to 1848, subsequently employed at the King Street works as a gilder and Japan painter.

*COCKER, GEORGE. Figure modeller first half nineteenth century. Later employed by Mintons, etc.

DEAKIN, H. Late nineteenth century.

DEAN, W. E. J. Scenic and marine painter. Late nineteenth century, early twentieth century.

GREGORY, A. Floral artist. Late nineteenth, early twentieth century. (Also Mintons.)

HANCOCK, H. S. Landscape artist, etc., King Street factory, *c.* 1880 into twentieth century.

HASLEM, JOHN. Born 1808, figure painter, *c.* 1822–40, d. 1884.

HOGG, H. WARRINGTON. Modeller, etc., from *c.* 1880 to his death in 1893.

HOLTZENDORF, COUNT. Landscape artist. Late nineteenth century.

INGRAM, W. R. Principal modeller from *c.* 1880.

JONES. Floral artist King Street factory.

LANDGRAFF, G. Figure painter, *c.* 1880–3, formerly employed by Brown-Westhead, Moore.

LEAD, LEONARD. Floral artist, *c.* 1805–40, d. 1869.

*LEROY, DESIRÉ. Floral and bird painter, *c.* 1890 into twentieth century, formerly at Mintons, d. 1908.

*LUCAS DANIEL, SENR. Born 1788. Landscape artist, *c.* 1830–48, d. 1867. His sons later employed at Copeland & Mintons.

MOSLEY, WILLIAM E. Floral artist, Osmaston Road and King Street factories, mainly twentieth century.

PLATTS, JAMES. Figure painter. Late nineteenth century.

PRINCE, EDWARD. Landscape artist, *c.* 1825–48, later for King Street factory.

*ROUSE, JAMES, SENR. Born 1802, apprenticed *c.* 1820. Coalport *c.* 1827–60. King Street factory *c.* 1875–82. Royal Crown Derby *c.* 1882–8, d. 1888.

ROUSE, JAMES, JUNR. Landscape artist. Late nineteenth century.

SLATER, WILLIAM. Fruit, insects, etc., also gilding, *c.* 1820–48, later at Davenports, d. 1864.

*STEELE, HORATIO. Floral artist, *c.* 1825–48, d. 1874 in the Potteries.

DERBY

*STEELE, THOMAS. Fruit and Floral artist, *c.* 1815–25 (later at Mintons), d. *c.* 1850.

WALE, JOHN P. Floral and scenic artist, from Worcester, *c.* 1878 into twentieth century. d. 1920.

WHITAKER, JOHN. Modeller, *c.* 1830–47.

DERBY MARKS

Mark No.

21 Normal form of "Crown Derby" mark before 1830.

22 Earliest form of Bloor period marks, *c.* 1820–40.

23 Bloor period mark, *c.* 1825–48.

24 Bloor period mark, *c.* 1830–48.

25 Mock Sèvres and Dresden marks occur during the Bloor period. The Dresden crossed swords mark was also used in the eighteenth and nineteenth centuries.

Mark No.

26 Locker & Co., *c.* 1848. Similar printed marks incorporating the names Stevenson Sharp, Hancock or Courtney occur *c.* 1848–59.

27 Stevenson & Hancock (King Street factory) mark used *c.* 1862 and continued by Sampson Hancock into the twentieth century.

28 Printed mark of the new Company, introduced about 1877 and continued in use until 1889. Various small year marks occur under the main mark from *c.* 1882 onwards. See Table A (page 79) for reconstructed key.
   The impressed mark "Derby", with or without crown above, also occurs.

29 Printed mark with addition of "Royal Crown Derby" used from 1890 into twentieth century. "England" added *c.* 1891. "Made in England" used in twentieth century. Year marks continued to be used under this mark. Table A (page 79) shows example on left to represent the year 1898.

DERBY 1–01

30 Impressed mark and date showing month and last two numbers of the year in which the piece was potted. Early twentieth century. The year is given in full after 1911.

DERBY

TABLE A

DERBY YEAR-CYPHERS, BELIEVED TO BE CORRECT
TO WITHIN ONE YEAR

1882	1883	1884	1885	1886	1887	1888
1889	1890	1891	1892	1893	1894	1895
1896	1897	1898	1899	1900	1901	1902
1903	1904	1905	1906	1907	1908	1909
1910	1911	1912	1913	1914	1915	1916
1917	1918	1919	1920	1921	1922	1923
1924	1925	1926	1927	1928	1929	1930
1931	1932	1933	1934	1935	1936	1937
1938 I	1939 II	1940 III	1941 IV	1942 V	1943 VI	1944 VII
1945 VIII	1946 IX	1947 X	1948 XI	1949 XII	1950 XIII	1951 XIV
1952 XV	1953 XVI	1954 XVII	1955 XVIII	1956 XIX	1957 XX	1958 XXI ETC

The cyphers listed (on page 79) give the key to Years of Manufacture. They are used in conjunction with marks Nos. 28 and 29 (see page 78).

The two "V" signs of 1905 and 1942 should not be confused. The 1905 mark includes the word "England" and that of 1942 the words "Made in England". The same applies to the "X" signs of 1902 and 1947.

DERBY PATTERN NUMBERS

BLOOR PERIOD pieces do not generally bear pattern numbers. Some low numbers do occur but they are generally painters' and gilders' marks.

The STEVENSON & HANCOCK wares made at the King Street factory seldom bear pattern numbers as the main traditional patterns were known by name i.e. "Old Crown Derby Witches", "Old Crown Derby Rose" etc.

Repetitive patterns from the new Osmaston Road factory were numbered progressively from 1878 onwards. By January 1900 the number had reached 6000. The *model* number (generally found impressed on vases and figures) reached by 1900, was 1276.

29
CROWN DERBY plate painted by James Rouse (signed on reverse). *c.* 1887. Diam. 9¼ in. Mark No. 28.

30
ROYAL CROWN DERBY vase, the panel painted by Desiré Leroy in white enamel on a dark blue ground. *c.* 1898. Ht. 8¼ in. Mark No. 29.

Page 81

31
Oval plaque painted by the early MINTON artist John Simpson. Signed and dated 1841. 3¾ in. × 2¾ in.

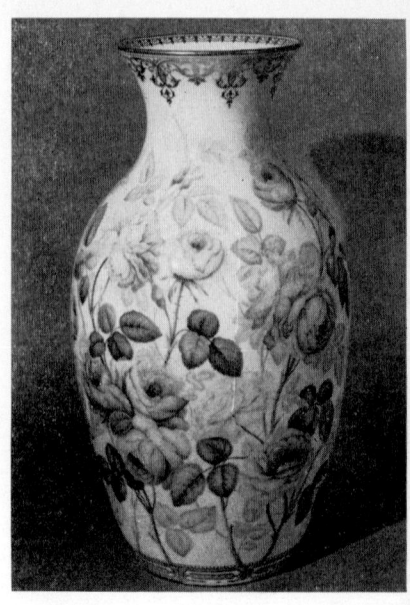

32
MINTON vase painted by Jesse Smith with continuous rose studies. *c.* 1850. Ht. 16 in. Mark No. 36.

33. Pair of MINTON tinted parian figures 'New Shepherd' and 'New Shepherdess'. *c.* 1851. Ht. 6¾ in.

Page 82

34
MINTON vase in the Sèvres style painted by Thomas Allen. 1851 Exhibition. Ht. 15 in. Mark No. 36. *Victoria & Albert Museum.*

35
MINTON vase, the figure panels painted by Thomas Allen. *c.* 1851. Ht. 20 in. *Minton Works Museum.*

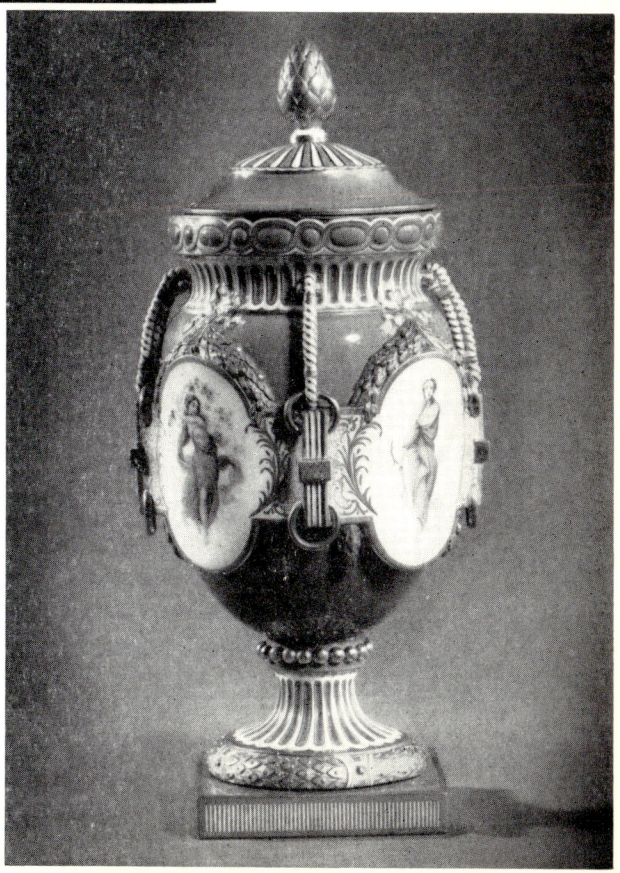

36. MINTON plate, a duplicate of part of the dessert service presented by Queen Victoria to the Emperor of Austria. 1851 Exhibition. *Victoria & Albert Museum.*

37
MINTON plate with pierced border. Panel showing the Foreign Nave at the 1851 Exhibition. *c.* 1851 (date cypher). Mark No. 37.

38
MINTON centrepiece in parian and porcelain designed by E. Jeannest. Duplicate of an 1851 exhibit. *c.* 1854. Ht. 27½ in. *Victoria & Albert Museum.*

39. MINTON celadon green vase, included in the 1862 Exhibition. Ht. 12 in. Mark No. 38. *Victoria & Albert Museum.*

40
MINTON vase painted by Louis Jahn in his Watteau style. 1862 Exhibition. Ht. 15 in. *Minton Works Museum.*

41
MINTON vase (one of a pair) in the Sèvres style, figure panels by Thomas Allen. Turquoise blue ground. 1862 Exhibition Ht. 16 in. Mark No. 39.

42. MINTON vase in imitation of a Chinese vase, signed by Léon Arnoux. 1862 Exhibition. Ht. 14¾ in. *Victoria & Albert Museum.*

CHAPTER 5

MINTON

THOMAS MINTON (1765–1836) was first apprenticed as an engraver to the Caughley factory and afterwards established himself as a master engraver in London where he made engravings for Adams, Wedgwood and Spode. He founded the Minton factory at Stoke-on-Trent in 1793 and when he died in 1836 his son, Herbert (1793–1858), carried on the concern in partnership with John Boyle under the title of Minton & Boyle until 1841. Accordingly we find the earliest Victorian pieces marked with various printed marks incorporating the initials M & B, while the wares of the following three years, that is from 1841 to 1844, may be marked "M & Co." Later marks are given on pages 116–118.

A large proportion of the early Minton wares were of transfer printed earthenware of fine quality and typical of their period in decoration and treatment. Thomas Minton always set a high standard and from 1825, he employed three of the foremost Derby painters. The work of these three artists, Joseph Bancroft, George Hancock and Thomas Steele is now extremely rare, and is mainly represented by some richly decorated large bowls and tea sets with reserve panels of floral composition on a dark blue ground enriched with gilt scrollwork.

It will be seen in Chapter 7 that Mintons were producing parian figures on a large scale towards the end of the 1840's, but some charming unglazed white figures and groups of a similar body were being produced earlier in that decade and in the 1830's. Like most products of this period they are difficult to identify.

In 1847 a writer in the *Art Union* was commenting on Minton's figures: "Minton's bisque figures are now superior to the French in artistic management of drapery, and particularly in the lace imitations and he gives equal excellence at a cheaper rate." An 1846 review explains the relatively simple method of obtaining the lace effects on these unglazed bisque figures: "The bisque figures of Messrs. Mintons have enjoyed for a long time a very considerable sale . . . they are most carefully executed, and were until lately, the very best productions of this class of art in the Potteries. The imitation of lace as an appendage to most of these figures, is here carried out very successfully, and causes a 'prettiness' and novelty that secure many purchasers. The process by which this is effected is extremely simple. Real lace is the groundwork which, being immersed in 'slip', becomes saturated, and a coat or crust, adheres to it, which in the firing becomes firm, while the lace is of course destroyed, leaving the pattern perfect in 'bisquet'" (*Art Union*, 1846).

It will have been apparent from the exhibition reviews quoted in Chapter 1, that Minton's porcelain had achieved a high reputation and this was due largely to the great number of well-known artists employed by the firm. This fact is stressed by a student who published anonymously a small work entitled *Pottery and Porcelain in 1876* in which he describes his rambles through the china shops of London in that year. This little-known booklet contains some interesting unprejudiced comments on the stocks of the leading manufacturers of the period. One of his numerous references to Mintons reads: "... In high class pottery Mintons are to the china trade what the light of the sun is to the earth. Withdraw the house of Mintons from the firmament and the other firms now existing would only supply the place of the moon and the stars. Potteries seem to have their rise, their day of glory, and their decline, and just now the star of Minton is in the ascendant. One reason why certain manufacturers excel others in artistic pottery is that they engage the best artists to decorate for them. Some small firms make very good china, but they hesitate about paying so very highly for the best talent, fearing they may not recoup themselves for their outlay. Messrs. Mintons have not hesitated to employ the best talent that come to their hand, and they have by this means succeeded in gaining for their house a prestige above that of any other English firm."

Mention has been made of the Derby trained artists, Bancroft, Hancock and Steele, but these artists were employed earlier than the period covered by this book. The first truly Victorian artist of whom we have record was John Simpson. L. Jewitt, in his *Ceramic Art of Great Britain* wrote in 1878: "Mr. John Simpson held the position of principal enamel painter of figures and the highest class decorations, from about 1837 to 1847, when he removed to London to take charge of the porcelain painting at Marlborough House." This statement has been repeated by subsequent writers, but is not entirely accurate, as in 1847 the Government School was situated at Somerset House and was not moved to Marlborough House until later.

The writer has been unable to identify any of Simpson's work on factory productions, but it was a common practice at this period for ceramic artists to augment their income by painting portrait miniatures on porcelain in their own time and these portraits often represent the only signed work of the artists. One such portrait plaque by Simpson dated 1841, is illustrated in Plate 31. John Simpson was born in 1811 and was the son of Mundy Simpson, a Derby gilder and "Japan" pattern painter. John learned the rudiments of this art from his father at Derby but he left there for the Potteries about 1830. From 1837 to 1847 he was employed at Mintons. The rest of his life was spent in London where he became a well-known enamel painter, examples of his work being included in Royal Academy Exhibitions from 1847 to 1871 with but two exceptions—1864 and 1866. John Simpson's son, William Page Simpson (b. 1845, d. 1911), who, like his father, was an enamel and ceramic artist, has on occasions been listed as a Minton artist. He is better known, however, for his work for the entirely separate tile firm of Minton Hollins and examples of his painting for this firm were shown at the Vienna Exhibition of 1873.

The year 1848 was to have far reaching consequences in the history of Mintons for in this year they engaged the French potter Léon Arnoux (b. 1816, d. 1902). The success of his appointment at Mintons had a great influence on many of his fellow countrymen who, as a result, followed him to England in later years. Léon Arnoux was both the Chemist and the Art Director at Mintons and was forever experimenting with new bodies, glazes and techniques. The "Majolica" ware with its coloured glazes over an earthenware body, which proved so popular at the 1851 Exhibition, was one of his early innovations and was to remain a stable product for most of the era, and there was scarcely any known type of ceramic decoration that Mintons did not attempt to emulate through their resourceful new Art Director. A rare signed copy of a Chinese crackleware vase (Plate 42) is preserved in the Victoria & Albert Museum and, were it not for the signature and mark, would be accepted by many collectors as oriental. Arnoux's services to the industry were recognised in 1878 when he was awarded the Order of Francis Joseph, and was made a Chevalier of the Legion of Honour for "his conspicuous success as a potter" and in recognition of his services in drawing up reports on the ceramic sections of the international exhibitions. A writer in the *Art Journal* stated that Arnoux "will always be remembered by Englishmen as among the most talented and accomplished Frenchmen who ever honoured our shores and aided us in the development of our Art Industries". He retired about 1895 but continued his association with Mintons up to the time of his death in 1902.

One of the first of the foreign ceramic artists to join Mintons was Christian Henk, a German by birth. Henk was employed from about 1848 and specialised in "Watteau"-style figures in landscapes and cupid subjects. While his work is of fine quality it is unsigned, as is the work of most artists at this relatively early period. Christian Henk died in 1905. His son, John (b. 1846, d. 1914), was employed by Mintons from 1863 and was responsible for some spirited animal models mostly carried out in "Majolica" glazed earthenware.

An early figure painter who took John Simpson's place was Thomas Allen (b. 1831). He was employed at Mintons while in his early teens and decorated some of the finest Minton pieces shown at the 1851 Exhibition, examples of which are preserved at the Victoria & Albert Museum and in the Minton Works Museum (see Plates 34, 35 and 41). Thomas Allen mainly painted Sèvres style figure panels on vases, but occasionally he painted floral compositions, a signed and dated example is preserved in the Victoria & Albert Museum. While employed at Mintons he spent his evenings studying at the Stoke-on-Trent School of Art and in 1852 was awarded the first National scholarship to the South Kensington School. He returned to Mintons in 1854. His fine figure painting was included in the various international exhibitions and was constantly praised. The vase illustrated in Plate 41 is one of a pair shown at the 1862 Exhibition and may be regarded as a typical example of Allen's style. Although he enjoyed such a wide reputation he seldom signed his work. Our anonymous student, writing in 1876, noted: "His painting was, to my idea, some of the best I saw." William Burton (*History and Description of English Porcelain*, 1902) referred to Allen as the "most skilful English figure painter on porcelain". In 1875 Thomas Allen joined Wedgwoods, his work for this firm being first shown at the Paris Exhibition of 1878. He retired about 1900 and died in 1915.

The Minton artists were fortunate to have at their head the enterprising Herbert Minton (b. 1793, d. 1858) whose influence on the firm is aptly summed up in the Juries Report on the 1862 Exhibition: "It would be difficult to estimate too highly the influence which his labours had in the advancement of English ceramic art—directly upon his own manufacture and indirectly upon the general products of that class of industrial art. From his own private resources and, at his own private risk, he originated and perfected works which rivalled the productions of Royal manufacturers favoured and stimulated by National subsidies." At the time of his death in 1858 the works gave employment to nearly fifteen hundred people. Herbert Minton was succeeded by his nephew Colin Minton Campbell who remained as Managing Director until his death early in 1885. Campbell's collection was sold at Christies in 1902 and included important specimens decorated by the leading Minton artists.

The 1862 vase already mentioned and shown in Plate 41 is typical of Mintons' Sèvres-styles wares; in this instance the ground colour alone proclaims its Minton origin. This is Mintons' rich glossy turquoise blue, a colour which when fired correctly was unequalled by any other factory. This particular blue was much used during the second half of the nineteenth century and proved most useful for the many classes of ware derived from Sèvres patterns. Thomas Kirkby was employed with Thomas Allen from 1845. Kirkby worked mainly as a figure painter on the "Majolica" glazed earthenware, although fine Sèvres-type porcelains were decorated by this artist, both with figure and floral motifs. He reputedly painted the floral panels on the dessert set given by Queen Victoria to the Emperor of Austria—(Plates 36 and 75). The former Sèvres figure painter Émile Lessore (b. 1805, d. 1876) was employed at Mintons for a brief period about 1858, but is mainly known for the charmingly free painting that he carried out on Wedgwood's creamware from 1859 to 1876. Edouard Rischgitz was a painter with a somewhat similar style who was employed by Mintons for decorating earthenware from about 1864 to 1870.

Louis H. Jahn came to England from Vienna in 1862 and was, like most of the foreign artists, first employed at Mintons, where he worked as a figure painter for a period of ten years before joining the firm of W. Brownfield as Art Director. In 1895 he returned to Mintons, and succeeded Léon Arnoux as Art Director. From 1900 until his death in 1911 Jahn was Curator of the Hanley Museum.

During his first ten-year engagement with Mintons he painted many Sèvres-type vases for international exhibitions. The *Art Journal* report of the 1871 Exhibition includes the following reference: "The vase with Cupids is a very fine specimen, remarkable for the softness and brilliancy of its colours. The decoration is original and Mr. Yahn, the artist, is entitled to great credit." Jahn's name was often given as Yahn in contemporary reports.

Of the Minton floral artists the best-known in the 1850's was Jesse Smith, the rose specialist. The simple vase with continuous rose studies illustrated in Plate 32 was probably painted by this artist, who seldom, if ever, signed his work. Jesse Smith later worked for Copelands. Other mid-nineteenth-century floral artists were Samuel Buxton, William Cooper, Aaron Green, John Latham, T. H. Simpson, Albert Slater and Joseph Wareham.

The charming mellow quality of Mintons' floral and other painting is due largely to the special soft glaze used on pieces decorated by the leading artists. This glaze, introduced in the 1851 period, allowed the added enamel colours partly to sink into and merge with the glaze instead of standing above the surface and producing the hard appearance to be seen on so many continental wares. Pieces treated with this special glaze bear, in addition to the normal factory mark, a small "ermine" mark (No. 36). In some cases this mark is incorporated with the factory mark, but it always denotes an example decorated by one of the foremost artists.

In 1863 Mintons introduced a method of acid gilding which, once seen, is unmistakable. The process involved eating away with acid those portions of the design intended to be left matt. The design was then gilt and, when burnished, the etched parts escaped the burnisher and remained matt in contrast to the highly burnished spots. Other firms later used this technique.

Of other Minton artists employed from the 1860's onwards, mention must be made of Henry Mitchell, Richard Pilsbury and Charles Toft. At this period the effects of the Government Schools of Design and Art was being felt in the ceramic industry. According to an 1863 census "fully two thirds of the numerous painters, gilders and modellers employed by them (Mintons) either are, or have been, students of the schools of Art" (*Art Journal*, 1864). Henry Mitchell was a talented animal painter whose best work is often signed. He worked from the early 1860's up to the 1890's.

Richard Pilsbury (b. 1830, d. 1897), a pupil of the local Burslem

School of Design where he won twelve National medals, was one of Mintons' most important floral artists from about 1866 to 1892, when he joined Moore Brothers as Art Director. He died in 1897. Richard Pilsbury's floral painting was based on gouache studies taken from nature, and was included in the many Victorian exhibitions. In later years he favoured studies of orchids. M. L. Solon, writing in the *Art Journal* (1897) remarked of his late colleague: "Pilsbury may be said to have witnessed the dawn of the new era which was to change the face of English decorative art and to have been one of those whose artistic work has materially assisted in bringing about the revolution in the public taste ... he turned to nature, the only guide which never misleads, and by his untiring work in the greenhouses, his conscientious reproductions of the best models he found there, he gained the experience and the skill he wanted to emerge from the swamp of the old routine and bud out as a true and complete flower painter."

Charles Toft, another instance of local talent, was born in 1831. He studied at the Stoke-on-Trent School of Design, and according to family tradition, he joined Mintons at the early age of fifteen, that is in 1845. This date is probably too early and may refer to his employment at Worcester. In the late 1860's he was instructor at the Birmingham School of Art and employed by Elkingtons, a firm famed for their silver and plated wares. He seems to have begun his employment at Mintons about 1872. He was a skilful modeller as various signed busts in parian prove but he is best known for his intricate and painstaking copies of the early French inlaid "Henri Deux" earthenware. Toft afterwards joined Wedgwoods as chief modeller, and in 1889 he established a small pottery at Stoke. He died in 1909. His son Albert Toft (b. 1862, d. 1949), who was employed at Wedgwoods, became a sculptor.

The early 1870's were momentous years for Mintons and the influx of foreign artists was accelerated. M. L. Solon who was to become the most celebrated ceramic artist of the era came to England in 1870 and introduced to this country the technique of *pâte-sur-pâte* decoration. A full account of Solon's career is given in Chapter 8. Another far-reaching event of this period was the employment of the already established designer and water-colour artist, William Stephen Coleman (b. 1829, d. 1904). Coleman had been employed for a brief period with Copelands but changed his allegiance to Mintons in 1869. The *Art Journal* of June contains the first reference to

Coleman's ceramic painting: "At McLean's Gallery in the Haymarket there is now exhibiting a collection of very remarkable works ... the productions of the well-known and highly esteemed artist, Mr. W. S. Coleman. They are paintings—not on paper or canvas, but on porcelain slabs, executed at the renowned manufactory of 'Minton', at Stoke-on-Trent. Each is from a design by Mr. Coleman, and the series does him great credit; it is very varied; the artist indulges a free fancy, and is graceful in all the compositions he thus presents to us; sometimes, indeed, he reaches high Art, and is never other than pleasing. ... We rejoice that a painter of so much ability has thus associated himself with an art for which comparatively little has been done in England by artists who are not absolutely educated to that branch of the profession. ..."

The anonymous student to whom reference has already been made, writing in 1876, relates that one of Coleman's plaques was valued at a hundred pounds. He also remarks that one of the figures was "... perhaps too nude but so good in drawing, and so innocently rendered, it could scarcely fail to please". Apart from his own ceramic paintings Coleman made many characteristic coloured drawings to be copied by Mintons' other artists on porcelain (Plate 43). G. W. Rhead who, as a young apprentice worked with Coleman, remarked that Coleman "produced a series of plaques, bowls, fireplace slabs etc. so charmingly fresh in character, so entirely different in treatment from anything previously seen in the Potteries, that they at once made a deep impression. ... Coleman's earliest work was done in underglaze colours upon the bisque and glazed by hand with the brush, not dipped. ... By this means he could distribute the glaze as he chose. The delicate parts of the painting, such as flesh and faces of figures, would be glazed thinly, while cobalt blue, which is a strong colour, requiring and absorbing more glaze, would be glazed more thickly. ... Coleman, however, who was a born colourist, and had a preference for the brighter pigments, became impatient of the somewhat limited range which underglaze colours afforded. He preferred the brilliant turquoise enamel (for which Mintons were famous) to the paler hues of the underglaze. ... He therefore gradually abandoned the use of underglaze colours, and his latest works were painted almost entirely in enamel colours with the exception of the strong brown outline, which was done in underglaze, and which was never abandoned, and occasionally one or two other colours, such as orange, which in underglaze is very brilliant" (*Staffordshire Pots and Potters*, 1906).

The *Art Journal*'s (1887) comments on Coleman's influence on English ceramics include the following reference: "we may attribute probably to him in some measure the broader treatment of English faience, of which examples were exhibited in Paris at the Exhibition of 1872. He, so to speak, set the pot painter's palette anew, and showed the way to a richer, juicier scheme of colour, which was yet essentially ceramic in character." Two of Coleman's sisters—Helen Cordelia Coleman (Mrs. Angell) and Rebecca Coleman—also decorated Minton's wares and would seem to have shared their brother's feeling for colour. The *Magazine of Art*'s report on a Howell & James' exhibition of ceramic paintings in 1884 commented on Rebecca Coleman's work: "The loss which this branch of china painting has sustained by the death of the latter is not easily over-estimated. In skill of handling, in the bright purity of her tints, she was unequalled. The last work of her which I have seen was like a rainbow."

In 1871 Mintons established a London Art Pottery Studio, a short-lived, little-known, but most interesting venture. W. S. Coleman was sent from Stoke to become Art Director at this studio, which employed and encouraged students from the Art Schools to decorate Mintons' wares in a new and unrestricted manner. The first notice concerning this novel scheme is contained in the *Art Journal* of December 1870. "Her Majesty's Commissioners for the Exhibition of 1851 have leased a plot of ground upon their Gore estate at South Kensington to Messrs. Minton and Co., of Stoke-on-Trent, whereon is now being erected an Art Pottery studio from the designs of Mr. Gilbert R. Redgrave. The management of this studio will be confided to Mr. W. J. [*sic*] Coleman, and he will select a few skilled painters from Stoke and students from the National Art Training Schools at Kensington, and conduct a class for practical china painting. A kiln, so arranged as to consume its own smoke, will be constructed, and it is hoped that, with its facilities, eminent artists (ladies especially) may be induced to paint upon porcelain and majolica."

G. W. Rhead, who had worked at the Kensington studio wrote: "The studio was established under the happiest auspices. No project, surely was ever launched with greater opportunities. It soon became one of the show places of London and was visited by a number of the most highly placed personages . . ." (*Staffordshire Pots and Potters*). The examples decorated at this studio normally bear the circular printed mark "Mintons Art-Pottery Studio Kensington Gore" (Mark No. 41) as well as the normal impressed "Minton" mark and date cypher. Of the many artists who received early training and recognition while employed there, mention must be made of A. B. Donaldson, Matthew Elden, John Eyre, Edward Hammond, Edmond G. Reuter and J. D. Rockfort.

Towards the end of 1873 Coleman gave up his post with Mintons and returned to painting in oil and water colour and to illustrating; and, from then onwards, the products of the Kensington studio lost much of their life and character. The studio was destroyed by fire during the summer of 1875 and was not rebuilt. An interesting contemporary account of this venture and the methods of decoration is contained in the *Art Journal* of 1872. It must be acknowledged that the majority of pieces decorated at this studio were pottery rather than porcelain.

To return to the parent factory at Stoke, we find that many continental artists had been engaged during the early 1870's. One of the most noteworthy was Antonin (or Anton) Boullemier. Boullemier was born at Metz about 1840 and studied in Paris where he was employed at various decorating establishments as well as at the Sèvres factory. In 1872 he came to England and was engaged by Mintons. He excelled in delicate, charming figure compositions, often of cupid subjects in the French style (Plate 44). His work is of fine quality and soon became widely known. Needless to say his work was exhibited in the international exhibitions and graced many of Mintons' more important commissions, often for Royalty. Antonin Boullemier also painted many portraits and miniatures and exhibited in the Royal Academy exhibitions of 1881 and 1882. The author is fortunate in having corresponded with Anton Boullemier's son, Henri, who from the age of thirteen, had worked with his father, "mixing, grinding and preparing his colours ready for him to start work at 8 a.m. prompt". Henri Boullemier relates that it was Solon, already successfully established at Mintons, who sent for Anton to join his French colleagues at Stoke. "Everything went on swimmingly for a time, all these men would come to the works in top hats, and white shirt fronts and as they could all of them sing well . . . many delightful moments were had by those near enough to hear them. Father had a very fine bass voice, he had been offered a position as principal bass at the Opéra-Comique in Paris, but preferred his artistic profession."

Henri Boullemier throws light on the circumstances that led to Boullemier establishing his own studio at his home in Stoke. "A day arrived when Colin Minton Campbell dared to criticise my father's work—that did indeed settle matters. My father tore up his contract, marched out and said 'Now you will send your work to my studio'. Having broken with Mintons he was free to decorate for other houses. He executed some wonderful work, including many exhibition pieces, for Brown-Westhead, Moore, but most of his time was still occupied on commissions for Mintons. Boullemier's painting was very popular in the United States, and, on his death, one large New York firm "despatched a special representative to this country . . . to contact my mother and purchase anything that he could find of works signed or unsigned by A. Boullemier".

The extent to which these foreign artists settled and became part of the social life of the Potteries can also be seen from Henri Boullemier's reminiscences. "He was always willing to sing at social gatherings; he had numerous pupils for singing lessons and as they developed he organised Concerts and Operatic performances. . . ." The Rhead brothers confirm this popularity. "It would be safe to say that in the whole of North Staffordshire no person was more generally known, or a greater favourite. . . . His work will always obtain for him an honourable position in English ceramics but he will be long remembered in Staffordshire for his personality alone . . ." (*Staffordshire Pots and Potters*). Boullemier died on April 25th, 1900. His sons Henri and Lucien also painted for Mintons in a similar style to that of their father.

Lucien Besche was employed in 1871, but soon left for Copelands (see Chapter 3). At this period Désiré Leroy joined Mintons. He reputedly received his training at the Sèvres factory and certainly painted exotic birds and floral motifs in the style associated with that factory. While employed at Mintons he was responsible for some very effective floral and bird studies in white enamel on a slightly tinted ground very much in the manner of *pâte-sur-pâte* decoration (Plate 45). Leroy continued to decorate for Mintons until 1890 when he left to take up the appointment of Art Director with the Royal Crown Derby Company, a position he held until his death in 1908.

In 1872 another French-trained artist joined Mintons, William

Mussill. He was originally at Sèvres, and at Mintons he painted flowers and birds in rich intense colours mostly on earthenware. Like C. F. Hürten of Copelands, he was a keen student of nature and spent much of his time in the conservatories at Trentham and elsewhere making gouache studies on tinted paper which were later used in the decoration of Mintons' wares. The paper studies were, like his ceramic paintings, signed W. Mussill—the first "s" being long giving a signature resembling Mupill. His work in the Paris Exhibition of 1878 has been mentioned in Chapter 1. Mussill trained a local artist Henry Penson (of whom a *Pottery Gazette* reporter predicted in 1890, "We shall come to be proud of Mr. Penson") to follow in his footsteps. William Mussill died in 1906.

During most of the second half of the nineteenth century Mintons were producing ambitious parian wares—ornate centrepieces and comports for richly painted porcelain dessert sets, candelabra, etc., as well as a large range of decorative figures. The reader is referred to Chapter 7 for a detailed account of this typically Victorian ceramic body.

Solon continued to work in *pâte-sur-pâte* decoration during the 1870's, 80's and 90's. The expense and time involved in this delicate process naturally restricted the number of examples available. The *Magazine of Art* noted that one vase, thirty-six inches high, took two and a half years to complete, "so it is not surprising that the vase is valued at 1500 guineas." A full account of this process, and of the apprentices trained by Solon, is contained in Chapter 8.

The cost of the more orthodox decoration was also high, especially when one bears in mind the comparatively low wages prevailing at this period. A single ornate Sèvres vase made for Queen Victoria in 1880 was priced at 240 guineas. This high cost of Victorian porcelain pieces is repeatedly emphasised in contemporary reports and was no doubt caused by the use of the finest materials in every department and by the international repute of the artists engaged in the decoration. Another source of great expense in the making of high quality porcelain was the loss incurred during the various firing processes. The most anxious moments were during the final firing when the most painstaking efforts of the artists could be irretrievably ruined if the heat of the kiln was not precisely controlled.

Returning to Mintons' ceramic artists who normally signed their work, attention must be drawn to J. E. Dean, H. W. Foster, E. G. Reuter and Albert Wright. J. E. (Teddy) Dean (d. 1935) started his career at Mintons in 1882, remaining with them for over forty years. Although, as one of his contemporaries has stated, "he could turn his hand to anything in painting on china" he is mainly known for his realistic animal, fish and game studies.

Herbert Wilson Foster (b. 1848, d. 1929) had joined Mintons in 1872 after early training at the Hanley School of Art and at South Kensington. He quickly built up a reputation as a figure artist specialising in portraits, often of Royalty or other well-known personalities. Occasionally he painted animal and bird subjects which show high finish and originality. H. W. Foster was one of several ceramic artists who exhibited at the Royal Academy exhibitions. He travelled to the Continent on many occasions and exhibited there. In 1893 he took up teaching at the Nottingham School of Art.

Edmond G. Reuter (b. 1845) was first associated with Mintons at their Kensington Gore Art Pottery Studio (page 97). He was employed at Stoke from about 1875 to 1895 and although the *Pottery Gazette* refers to him in 1886 as assistant designer to Arnoux, the Art Director, his undoubted talents do not seem to have been recognised or used to the full. The son of a botanist, Reuter inherited a love for plants and later studied floral design in Paris. In 1868 he visited Egypt and became aware of the richness of oriental art, a source of design that was to influence his later work. After over twenty years in England Edmond Reuter returned in 1895 to his native Switzerland, where be became well-known as a water-colour painter and designer.

Albert Wright joined Mintons about 1871. He was a popular painter of birds and fish and continued working into the twentieth century. His work was in great demand in the United States of America and is normally found on richly gilt plates with delicate ground colours (Plate 46), and on some of these he occasionally depicted other subjects; an example in the Minton Works Museum has a centre panel of a hunting scene. He normally signed his work with the initials A.H.W. which were often scratched through a dark foreground tint.

Mintons were among the few ceramic manufacturers to be noticeably influenced by the Art Nouveau style of decoration which was in vogue during the closing years of the Victorian era. The lead in this direction was given by Léon Solon (born 1872) who received early training at the Hanley School of Art and, like many ceramic designers, graduated by way of a National Scholarship to the South Kensington School. *The Studio* contained many references to Léon Solon during the 1890's and illustrated several designs by him. The first reference to his employment at Mintons is contained in *The Studio* 1896: "There are not many South Kensington students who make a reputation as designers before they complete their course in Schools. . . . And now that he is associated with Messrs. Minton, a firm with whom his father has been so long connected, it is pleasant to see that the master of *pâte-sur-pâte* has a worthy successor in other branches of applied art. . . ."

Léon Solon himself painted a series of wonderfully drawn plaques combining many different and novel styles of ceramic decoration, such as coloured slips, acid treatment and sgraffito work. As *The Studio* noted in 1890, "Mr. Solon is an untiring experimenter and, with the resources at his command, is likely to develop to its utmost capacity the possibilities of the craft to which he is devoted." As Art Director and designer at Mintons, he introduced many simple, but pleasing, designs ranging from printed motifs to majolica wares with raised slip motifs. He also made a reputation in many other fields—his bookbinding earned him commissions from Queen Victoria. In 1909 he emigrated to the United States of America and made his mark in that country, as he did here, in a number of fields. He was responsible for the colouring of architectural details and sculpture on the Museum of Fine Arts in Philadelphia, and the Rockefeller Centre, in New York. He was also known as a writer on architectural subjects and as a painter of landscapes and portraits. He died in Florida in 1957.

While this volume is concerned only with porcelain, it must not be forgotten that this comprised only part of Mintons' output. Their "Majolica" glazed earthenware and Palissy wares were also gaining an international reputation. Certainly to contemporaries the achievements of Mintons seemed widely based. "They have never been excelled by any firm at any time in resourcefulness leading to complete success in new departures of ceramics. There is scarcely a branch of pottery manufacture which they have not made their own" (*Art Journal*, 1896).

MINTON CERAMIC ARTISTS

* Artist given fuller mention in the text.

*ALLEN, THOMAS. Born c. 1831. Figure painter employed c. 1845–75. Subsequently Wedgwoods, d. 1915.
*ARNOUX, LÉON. Born 1816. Art Director, 1848–95, d. 1902.
BANCROFT, JOSEPH. Floral artist, c. 1840–57. Formerly at Derby and Copelands, d. 1857.
BAYLEY, E. S. Fish and bird painter, c. 1890–1905.
BELL, JOHN. The sculptor, modelled Parian figures, etc., c. 1845–60.
*BESCHE, LUCIEN. From France, c. 1871. Later at Copelands.
BIRBECK, WILLIAM. Bird painter.
BIRKS, ALBOIN. *Pâte-sur-pâte*, pupil of Solon, c. 1876–1937, d. 1941.
BIRKS, LAWRENCE A. *Pâte-sur-pâte*, pupil of Solon, c. 1876–95.
*BOULLEMIER, ANTONIN. Born c. 1840. Employed 1872 onwards. Celebrated figure painter, d. 1900.
BOULLEMIER, LUCIEN. Born 1876. Figure painter, early twentieth century, d. 1949.
BOURNE, SAMUEL. Chief designer, etc., c. 1828–63.
BUXTON SAMUEL. Mid-nineteenth century. Floral, fruit painter, etc.
CARRIER, ALBERT ERNEST (Carrier de Belleuse). French sculptor, modelled for Mintons, d. 1887.
COCKER, GEORGE. Figure modeller from Derby, c. 1853 onwards, d. 1868.
COLEMAN, HELEN CORDELIA. Floral work at Mintons' London Art Pottery Studio, c. 1872.
*COLEMAN, REBECCA. Figure subjects, c. 1870–80.
*COLEMAN, WILLIAM STEPHEN. Art Director and painter at London Art Pottery Studio, c. 1870–73.
COMELERA, PAUL. French modeller of animals, birds, etc., c. 1870–80.
COOPER, WILLIAM. Floral artist, c. 1860–85.
CRANE, WALTER, R.W.S. Born 1845. Designer, c. 1870, d. 1915.
*DEAN, J. E. (TEDDY). Animal painter, etc., from c. 1882 into twentieth century, d. 1935.
DONALDSON, A. D. Decorated at Mintons' London Studio. c. 1872.

DUDLEY, M. Floral artist, etc. Late nineteenth century, early twentieth century.

ELDEN, MATTHEW. London Studio, c. 1874.

EVANS, JOHN BISHOP. Landscape and marine views, c. 1865–85.

EYRE, GEORGE. Born 1816. Figure designs, c. 1847. d. 1887.

EYRE, JOHN. Born 1847. Mintons' London Studio, c. 1872. (Also Copelands and Doultons (Lambeth).) d. 1927.

*FOSTER, H. W. Born 1848. Figure painter, c. 1872 onwards, d. 1929.

GOODE, W. J. Amateur painter on Minton wares, c. 1865–90.

GREEN, AARON. Landscape, floral painter, etc., 1850–95, d. 1897.

GREGORY, A. Floral artist, c. 1890. (Subsequently at Derby.)

GREY, GEORGE. Decorator, c. 1860.

HAMMOND, EDWARD. Decorator, London Studio, c. 1873.

HANCOCK, GEORGE (?). Fruit and flowers, c. 1836, d. 1850.

HEATH, C. Figures, birds, etc., c. 1875.

*HENK, CHRISTIAN. Figure painter, 1842 onwards, d. 1905.

HENK, JOHN. Born 1846. Modeller. Employed from 1863, d. 1914.

HOLLINS, H., *Pâte-sur-pâte* artist. c. 1870–80.

JAHN, LOUIS H. Ceramic painter from 1862–72. Art Director, 1895–1900, d. 1911

JEANNEST, EMILE. Born 1813. Sculptor, designer, etc., c. 1845–52, d. 1857.

*KIRKBY, THOMAS. Born 1824. Figure subjects (often on "Majolica" wares). Also floral work, c. 1845–87, d. 1890.

LATHAM, JOHN. Floral artist, etc. Mid-nineteenth century. (Also Coalport.)

*LEROY, DÉSIRÉ. Born 1840. Floral and bird painter often in white enamel, c. 1874–90. Later at Derby, d. 1908.

LESSORE, EMILE. Figure subjects, c. 1858, subsequently at Wedgwoods, d. 1876.

LOCKETT, BENJAMIN. White enamel motifs, c. 1850–60.

LONGMORE, THOMAS. Modeller, c. 1865–85.

MARKS, HENRY STACEY. Born 1829. Designer—figure subjects, c. 1870–80, d. 1898.

MELLOR, T. *Pâte-sur-pâte* motifs, c. 1870.

MILES. *See* SOLON, M. L.

MITCHELL, HENRY. Animal, bird painter, etc., c. 1860–c. 72.

MORGAN, A. *Pâte-sur-pâte* motifs, c. 1870.

43
MINTON plate, the central panel painted by A. Boullemier after a design by W. S. Coleman.
c. 1872 (date cypher).
Mark No. 43.

44
MINTON vase (one of a pair), the season panels painted by A. Boullemier.
c. 1871 (date cypher).
Ht. 19 in. Mark No. 38A.

45

MINTON seau (one of a pair) decorated in white enamel on a turquoise blue ground by Desiré Leroy. *c.* 1876 (date cypher). Ht. 9 in. Mark MINTONS (impressed).

46

MINTON plate, yellow ground, the central panel painted by A. H. Wright. *c.* 1876.

47
MINTON plate with pierced border. The figure subject panel painted by A. Boullemier. *c.* 1884 (date cypher). Mark No. 43.

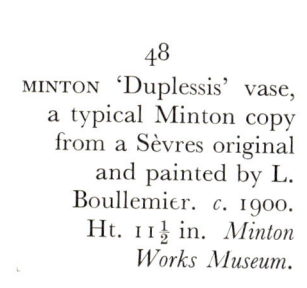

48
MINTON 'Duplessis' vase, a typical Minton copy from a Sèvres original and painted by L. Boullemier. *c.* 1900. Ht. 11½ in. *Minton Works Museum.*

Page 107

49. CHAMBERLAIN (WORCESTER) vase, richly gilt. *c.* 1840. Ht. 18⅜ in. Mark No. 47. *Victoria & Albert Museum.*

Page 108

50. KERR & BINNS (WORCESTER) comport from the 'Shakespeare' service shown at the Dublin Exhibition of 1853. Ht. 15½ in. *Worcester Works Museum.*

51
KERR & BINNS (WORCESTER) dish painted by Thomas Bott in white enamel on a rich blue ground. c. 1857. Diam. 9½ in. Mark No. 53.

52
KERR & BINNS (WORCESTER) dish decorated in 'Limoges enamel' style by Thomas Bott. c. 1858. Diam. 6½ in. Mark No. 53.

53. ROYAL WORCESTER. Replicas of the Dudley déjeuner service, showing the Worcester 'jewelling', gilding by S. Ranford, classical head panels by Thomas Callowhill. *c.* 1865. *Worcester Works Museum.*

54
ROYAL WORCESTER. The 'Ormond Vase', portraits of Ann Boleyn and her father (Earl of Ormond) painted in colour on a gold ground by Thomas Bott. *c.* 1868. Ht. 8½ in. Mark No. 55.

55
ROYAL WORCESTER Vase and cover painted by J. Rushton. 1870 (Factory date mark.) Ht. 14¾ in. Mark No. 55.

Page 112

*Mussill, W. Floral and bird compositions often on coloured body, 1872 onwards, d. 1906.
Palm. Cloisonné patterns, c. 1870–80.
Penson, Henry S. Born 1868. Floral artist. Pupil of Mussill, c. 1890, d. 1951.
*Pilsbury, Richard. Born c. 1830. Floral artist, c. 1866–92. Later Art Director Moore Brothers, d. 1897.
Pratt, H. L. Born 1805. Landscape artist from Derby, c. 1830–45, d. 1873.
Protat, Hughes. Modeller, designer, etc. Mid-nineteenth century. Also Wedgwoods.
Pugin, A. W. N. Designs, c. 1849–52.
Randall, G. Sèvres-style floral and bird painter, c. 1860.
*Reuter, E. G. Born 1845. Floral and figure designs, c. 1875–95.
Rhead, Frederick. *Pâte-sur-pâte*, etc., c. 1870–77. Later at Wedgwoods and Art Director at Brownfields.
Rice, T. H. *Pâte-sur-pâte* artist, c. 1870.
*Rischgitz, Edouard. Figure subjects chiefly on earthenware, c. 1864–70.
Rivers, L. Floral artist. Late nineteenth century, early twentieth century.
Roberts, Ellis. Born c. 1860. Figure painter, c. 1874–82, d. 1930.
Rouchard, Francois. Figure painter in slip technique, c. 1880.
Sanders, H. *Pâte-sur-pâte* artist, c. 1870. Later at Moore Bros.
Simpson, Aaron. Gilder of fine Sèvres-type vases. Late nineteenth century.
Simpson, John. Born c. 1811. Figure subjects, c. 1837–47, d. 1884.
Simpson, T. H. Floral and fruit artist. Mid-nineteenth century.
Slater, Albert. Floral artist, c. 1860. Later on Minton Hollins tiles.
Slater, Joseph. Born 1812. From Derby. Enamel painter, c. 1860–70. Later Brown-Westhead, Moore.
*Smith, Jesse. Floral artist, roses, etc. Mid-nineteenth century.
Smith, Moyr. Designer, etc., c. 1875.
*Solon, M. L. Born 1835. *Pâte-sur-pâte* decoration. 1870–1904, d. 1913 (see Chapter 8).
*Solon, Léon V. Born 1872. Art Director and decorator, c. 1897–1909. Figure subject plaques, etc., d. 1957.

STEELE, EDWIN. Born c. 1803. Floral and fruit painter. Trained at Derby, d. 1871.

STEELE, THOMAS. Born 1772. Floral and fruit artist from Derby, c. 1825–43, d. 1850.

STEVENS, ALFRED. Born 1817. Designs for Minton, c. 1860, d. 1875.

STEWART, R. Floral artist.

THOMAS, JOHN. Sculptor and modeller. Mid-nineteenth century.

*TOFT, CHARLES. Born c. 1831. Reproductions of "Henri Deux" inlaid wares. Also worked for Kerr & Binns, Wedgwoods and on his own account, d. 1909.

*TURNER, MISS ALICE. Figure painter, c. 1873–80.

WALKLETT, R. Floral artist. Late nineteenth century, early twentieth century.

WAREHAM, JOSEPH. Floral and bird subjects. Mid-nineteenth century.

*WRIGHT, ALBERT H. Bird, fish, etc. Late nineteenth century.

WYSE, WILLIAM. Designer, etc., c. 1875–85.

YAHN. See JAHN, LOUIS H.

MINTON MARKS

A system of year cyphers and month letters was used on Minton ware from 1842, see page 115. It was continued right through into the twentieth century. The year cypher, the month letter and the potter's mark (this last being the personal mark of the individual potter responsible for the particular piece) were impressed together to form a group of three.

For twenty years from 1842 these groups of three were often the only marks used. Then in 1862 the name MINTON was added to the group, followed ten years later, by MINTONS. The impressed cyphers relate to date of potting, not of decoration.

KEY TO MONTH LETTERS

J (January)   F (February)   M (March)   A (April)
E (May)   I (June)   H (July)   Y (August)
S (September)   O (October)   N (November)   D (December)

MINTON

Mark 31.   KEY TO YEAR CYPHERS   115

116 VICTORIAN PORCELAIN

Mark No.

32 Early porcelain mark before 1830, often with pattern number below.

33 Various ornate printed marks occur, incorporating the initials—

M	*c.* 1822–36
M & B	*c.* 1836–41
M & Co	*c.* 1841+
M & H	*c.* 1845+

and often with "Felspar china" on porcelain, and the pattern number.

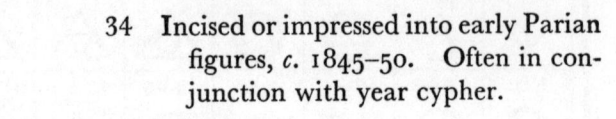

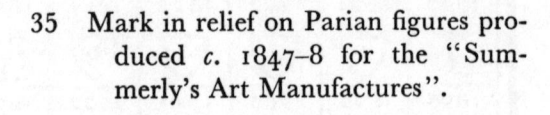

34 Incised or impressed into early Parian figures, *c.* 1845–50. Often in conjunction with year cypher.

35 Mark in relief on Parian figures produced *c.* 1847–8 for the "Summerly's Art Manufactures".

36 Painted "Ermine" mark *c.* 1850 onwards, indicating a special soft glaze. The "Ermine" mark with or without the addition of the letter "M" was occasionally used as a factory mark in the 1850's.

37 Printed mark, *c.* 1851.

MINTON 38*a* "Minton" impressed from *c.* 1862.

MINTONS 38*b* "S" added, *c.* 1872.

MINTON

Mark No.

39 Printed mark, *c.* 1860–70 occurs on 1862 Exhibition vases.
Special marks were used from time to time on specimens intended for international exhibitions.

40 Printed "Globe" mark, *c.* 1863–72, in this case incorporating the name of the London retailer, Thomas Goode & Co. Similar marks were used with the names of other retail firms.

41 Printed mark used at Mintons' London "Art-Pottery Studio", *c.* 1871–75.

42 Impressed "Colin Minton Campbell" mark, incorporating the date—1878. *c.* 1868–80. This mark occurs on fine copies of Sèvres vases, etc.

43 Crown added to printed "Globe" mark, and "S" added to "Minton", *c.* 1872.

44 Printed mark on specimens ordered by Goode & Co., *c.* 1875.

Mark No.

45 "England" added to printed "Globe" mark, *c.* 1891.

46 "Made in England" added, *c.* 1902. Laurel leaves added at sides of Globe mark, *c.* 1912.

MINTON PATTERN NUMBERS

The first series of Minton pattern numbers ran consecutively from 1 to 9999. Of these, approximately the first 800 were pre-1830 and were used in conjunction with Mark No. 32 (page 116). By the late 1830's the pattern numbers had climbed to 4000, and by 1849 they were in the 9000's.

A new series bearing the prefix "A" was started in 1850 which was discontinued in 1867 when the pattern number had reached A.7716.

Sample dates of "A" series. (*1850 to c. 1867*)

A.365 introduced in 1852
A.3082   ,,   ,, 1856
A.4604   ,,   ,, 1859
A.6080   ,,   ,, 1863
A.6584   ,,   ,, 1864
The "A" series ended at 7716

The "A" series was followed in 1868 by the "G" series which continued to operate until the end of the century.

Sample dates of "G" series. (*1868 to c. 1900*)

G.22 introduced in 1868
G.390   ,,   ,, 1870
G.982   ,,   ,, 1872
G.1533   ,,   ,, 1874
G.1815   ,,   ,, 1874
G.2078   ,,   ,, 1876
G.3314   ,,   ,, 1879
G.4512   ,,   ,, 1881
G.5147   ,,   ,, 1882

The "G" series did not apply to all Minton wares. It was restricted to porcelain breakfast, dinner, dessert, tea and coffee services bearing some gilt ornamentation in the design. Other prefixes were used to denote particular Minton products. As follows:

"B" Decoration without gilt enrichments, *c.* 1870 onwards.
"C" Earthenware, *c.* 1860 onwards.
"D" Toilet wares, *c.* 1860 onwards.
"E" Earthenware, *c.* 1870 onwards.
"O" Ornaments, *c.* 1848 to *c.* 1896.
"OA" Ornaments, *c.* 1896 onwards.
"P" Very richly decorated wares, *c.* 1873 to *c.* 1889.
"PA" Very richly decorated wares, *c.* 1889 onwards.

The "H" series was started about 1900. All pieces bearing an "H" pattern number may be regarded as twentieth-century productions.

It should be noted that some of the finest specimens of all periods do not bear pattern numbers as they were individual examples or were special commissions not to be repeated.

As a general rule the impressed date cyphers (page 115) afford a more reliable guide to the dating of Minton wares.

CHAPTER 6

WORCESTER

THE opening of the Victorian era coincided with the final years of Flight, Barr & Barr (1813–1840), the firm of Worcester porcelain makers which, under various titles, had continued the Worcester tradition from the Dr. Wall period. The three years prior to the firm's amalgamation with the Chamberlain factory in 1840 is of little interest to the student of Victorian ceramics for the patterns, shapes and general styles hardly varied from those employed during the 1820's.

CHAMBERLAIN

In 1840 a joint stock company was formed with a capital of £40,000 for the purpose of uniting the Flight, Barr & Barr company with that of the Chamberlain company which had been established at Worcester since the 1780's. With the experience of both companies working together under one roof, success seemed assured, but the absence of the old rivalry between the two firms resulted in a general decline in the standards of workmanship and the sporadic new innovations that were tried out were not very successful.

A large proportion of the works was given over to the manufacture of door furniture, but this venture failed to show financial or other reward. "The next introduction was scarcely more worthy of the attention of the Royal Porcelain Works, the manufacture, namely, of buttons; as an accessory, any department of potting which would be profitable might with propriety be introduced, but we fear that the button trade ... absorbed more time than was profitable and engaged attention which ought to have been devoted to the more legitimate works of the Manufactory." So wrote R. W. Binns in his book *Worcester Pottery and Porcelain 1751–1851*. Chamberlains were also unfortunate in that they ran into a costly lawsuit resulting from their acknowledged infringement of a patent for making tiles and buttons of dry clay moulded by pressure.

Examples of Chamberlain porcelain shown at the Manchester Exhibition of 1845–6 include a scent bottle with raised floral motifs;

a covered vase with applied griffin handles and knob, the body painted with flowers; a fluted Chinese-pattern covered teabowl and saucer; an "Etruscan"-pattern gilt jug; and a covered footed bowl with openwork decoration, of which the *Art Union* correspondent wrote ". . . it is one of a class which we have not seen produced elsewhere—a sort of network covering the form. There are other objects of the kind, which seem as if one were enclosed in another, where there is no obvious separation and it is the result of much labour in the piercing—with the finest and most delicate tools". This class of pierced porcelain originally produced in 1845 was to become a traditional style in the Worcester factories throughout the Victorian period.

As a result of their many difficulties the original Chamberlain partners, with the exception of Walter Chamberlain and John Lilly, retired in 1848; and in 1850 John Lilly also retired and was replaced by his son Frederic and by W. H. Kerr. Although Kerr soon made many improvements in the general factory arrangements, the benefits were not in time to be appreciated at the 1851 Exhibition. As we saw in Chapter 1 the Chamberlain exhibits could not compete with those of their rivals in the trade and this fact must have been apparent even before the exhibition opened, for, included in their display, were many examples from earlier and happier days. The failure of the Chamberlain Company at this all-important exhibition was to have far reaching consequences. Walter Chamberlain and Lilly retired leaving the energetic Kerr to continue the business. Kerr invited R. W. Binns to join him and to form a completely new company—generally known as Kerr & Binns—with Binns to act as Art Director infusing new ideas and directing the training of fresh young talent.

KERR & BINNS

On the formation of the Kerr & Binns company in 1852 the continuance of the Worcester tradition was assured. R. W. Binns described the new policy in his book *Worcester China 1852–97* ". . . it was to exalt the name and enhance the reputation of Worcester porcelain that the new proprietors applied themselves. They felt at the same time that if this work were to be accomplished it must be upon new lines; to revive old styles by old hands would neither show progress or meet the requirements of a newly educated and critical public, a change was imperative".

The first opportunity afforded to Kerr & Binns to compete with established manufacturers occurred at the Dublin Exhibition of 1853. A fine dessert service, the comports with parian figure supports depicting characters from Shakespeare's *A Midsummer Night's Dream* was designed and modelled by the young sculptor W. B. Kirk (Plate 50). The portrait panels were painted by Thomas Bott, who was soon to be well known for his copies of Limoges enamels. This service was most successful and did much to establish the large trade that Kerr & Binns were to enjoy in Ireland.

Many young artists were employed by the firm in its efforts to introduce fresh ideas and several had been trained at the Worcester School of Design. Thomas Bott was engaged in 1853. Born in 1829 he received his early training as a painter at the glassworks of W. H., B. & J. Richardson at Wordsley, near Stourbridge and some of his painted glass was apparently included in the 1851 Exhibition. Upon joining the Worcester company he was employed on the Shakespeare service and, in the following year, he was working on the decoration of the first of the Worcester porcelains in the Limoges style.

These "Limoges enamels", as they were called, were painted with a semi-opaque white enamel on a deep rich blue ground, giving a striking cameo-like effect (Plates 51, 52, 56 and 57). They were called "Limoges" because their style was suggested by the Renaissance painted enamel work on copper which was carried out at Limoges. Early examples of the Worcester Limoges enamels were shown to the Prince Consort who was enthusiastic in his praise, and later, when opening the Royal collection for Binns inspection is reported to have said: "Let your artists study the works of the Old Masters and, when they have become imbued with their spirit, let them design for themselves". Queen Victoria was later to continue the Royal patronage of the factory, the "Worcester enamels" being a favourite present of hers for members of the Royal Family.

The Paris International Exhibition of 1855 was a useful opportunity for Worcester porcelain to recuperate its reputation after the mediocre display at the 1851 Exhibition. The *Art Journal* report of the 1855 Exhibition included these comments: "Messrs. Kerr & Binns have recently produced some examples of the art of porcelain decoration, of which it is not too much to say that they surpass all the productions of this class that have been hitherto manufactured in the country. We allude chiefly to their attempts to imitate the artistic character of the works of Limoges on a porcelain body."

The *Art Journal* of 1857 contained the following reference to Bott's Limoges enamels: "The production of such works will necessarily be limited, from the peculiar talent necessary to their manipulation and we are gratified to learn that commissions have lately been given to an extent beyond the immediate capabilities of the manufacturers to supply. . . . We are glad to perceive that Her Majesty has already conferred valuable appreciative patronage upon these productions. The studies for the earliest of these works were lent to Messrs. Kerr & Binns by Sir Alfred Lechmere, who has been their constant and liberal patron. The famous collection of General the Hon. Edward Lygon was also placed at the service of the manufacturers, who have now also in progress copies of some of the celebrated 'enamels' belonging to Henry Danby Seymour Esq., M.P. kindly lent by that gentleman for the purpose. The figures and arabesques of Raphael, together with studies from Flaxman, form the leading features of the designs generally combined with such accessories and such originality of treatment as impart a character of novelty as well as beauty. The introduction of the 'gilding' is in extremely good taste. It is delicately applied and instead of being 'burnished' in the ordinary manner, is merely relieved by 'chasing'."

Besides this prestige work care was also given to the standard utilitarian productions; new shapes of elegant design were introduced, as were also new ground colours. A writer in the *Art Journal* of 1856 noted that the new management had already established a good reputation for all its productions, "from those of the highest and most costly character down to articles for ordinary and daily use".

Young artists were employed in every department. Josiah Rushton proved to be a popular figure painter. Joseph Williams painted rustic figures and landscapes in the style of Birket Foster. Robert Perling devoted himself to animal subjects. Bird subjects were painted by James Bradley, John Hopewell and James Weaver. Floral motifs were the speciality of Baker, David Bates and James Sherriff. The brothers James and Thomas Callowhill painted decorative heads and ornamentation often in Bott's enamel technique. The chased, matt and burnished gilding was of good quality and was used with restraint and good taste; most of it was the work of Josiah Davis and Samuel Ranford.

Some charmingly modelled parian figures and groups were produced, and also some rare figures finished in imitation of ivory and oxydised silver. A new body known as Raphaelesque porcelain was introduced about 1860 and its delicate tones were especially suited to the so-called "Capo di Monte" wares with their coloured relief motifs.

For the firm's finest productions a printed shield-shaped mark was used. This mark (No. 53) incorporates the last two figures of the year (which are often indistinct) and provides a space at the bottom left-hand corner for the artist to affix his signature or initials. Thomas Bott normally used his initials T. B. conjoined. The usual factory mark consists of a circle incorporating four cursive "W's" with a crescent containing the figure "51" in the centre. This mark, with the addition of a crown, was retained by the new Worcester Royal Porcelain Company in 1862 and is used to this day. Other marks incorporating the title "W. H. Kerr & Co" were occasionally used. In many contemporary reviews the firm is referred to as "Messrs. Kerr & Co." no reference being made to Binns.

In 1862 W. H. Kerr retired and returned to his native Ireland, and R. W. Binns on June 24th formed a new joint stock company under the title of the Worcester Royal Porcelain Company.

The work of the Kerr & Binns company during the ten years of its existence from 1852 to 1862, was remarkable for the interest it aroused among contemporaries. The period was short enough for the Kerr & Binns productions to have to-day a certain rarity value; and the finest documentary pieces, bearing the shield mark and date, combine the collector's requirements of quality and rarity.

ROYAL WORCESTER

When the new company was formed in 1862 production was at first confined to the general styles in favour under the Kerr & Binns management. Although Thomas Bott was mainly occupied with the Limoges enamels he was also painting in full colours (Plate 54). The Royal Worcester company was, however, soon to lose this artist whose work had been so important in raising the reputation of Worcester porcelain, for he died in 1870 at the early age of forty-one. One of his last works was a pair of vases and a ewer and stand illustrating the Norman Conquest which he painted from designs by the painter Daniel Maclise. These vases were exhibited at the South Kensington International Exhibition of 1871 and at Vienna in 1873, and are now to be found at the Worcester Works Museum (Plate 57). The ewer and stand is illustrated in Plate 56.

Thomas Bott's son, Thomas John Bott (b. 1854, d. 1932) was employed at the Worcester factory for some years where he painted in the style popularised by his father. He later became Art Director at the Coalport Works. The other Kerr & Binns' artists mentioned above continued to decorate Royal Worcester wares. The new company was fortunate in receiving a commission to make a presentation service commemorating the marriage of the Prince of Wales to Princess Alexandra in 1863. A similar presentation service was made for the Countess of Dudley in 1865. This service was richly gilt and jewelled by Samuel Ranford and reserve panels of classic female heads were painted by Thomas Callowhill. Duplicate pieces were later produced and can now be seen in the Worcester Works Museum (Plate 53). A single cup and saucer of this pattern was bought for fifty guineas in 1873 by the Earl of Dudley.

About 1870 the Worcester factory began to experiment with the new "Japanese" style which was becoming fashionable in nearly all the decorative arts. Under the direction of R. W. Binns a distinctively Worcester version of the Japanese style was evolved, using the ivory body which had been introduced ten years before. Early examples of this work were included in the South Kensington Exhibition of 1871 and in the Vienna Exhibition of 1873. The Japanese designs quickly caught the attention of the public and gave the Worcester modeller James Hadley an opportunity to show his talents. The quality of Hadley's modelling combined with the fine gilding of the Callowhill brothers enabled the Worcester factory to keep the lead in the use of this style in spite of the competition of other manufacturers.

The main impact of the Worcester Japanese work was made at the Vienna Exhibition of 1873. At this exhibition the Worcester company tied with Mintons for the highest award. One critic of the exhibition wrote, "We must all feel glad that a Works so renowned as the Worcester factory has again taken its legitimate place amongst the chief potters of the world; but what is most interesting in view of our present consideration, is the fact that all the finest of the Worcester works have been suggested by Oriental examples, and chiefly by works in Japanese lacquer; but the application is both new and clever" (*Art Journal*, 1873). It should perhaps be stressed that these Japanese wares were not imitative in the sense that they were copies of original pieces. "He (Binns) has seen and appreciated the value of Japanese art and . . . he has improved where he has borrowed, taking suggestion rather than models" (*Art Journal*, 1872). These remarks would apply equally to the other styles which influenced later Worcester—Persian, Italian and Indian.

The display of Worcester porcelain in the Japanese taste at the Vienna Exhibition of 1873 produced the following comments in the *Art Journal*: "Unique in design, quaint, without losing a certain eccentric beauty, it is, however, one of these fabrics that owe more to the original beauty of the material than even any subsequent embellishment. The difficulty of manufacture would seem to be considerable—notably in the case of statuettes, half a dozen failures occurring before a faultless work is produced. This once overcome, the peculiar ivory appearance is given by a warm, almost cream tinted enamel, the process of firing being stopped at an intermediate stage between biscuit and glaze . . . an elephant in ivory and bronze, alike quaint and pretty, would seem to be carved from an ivory tusk, and mounted on its brazen stand by some Oriental artist. There are many vases of various shapes, designed by Hadley; an octagonal pair decorated with the story of the silkworm in bronze and gold, and a series of six—a pair of pilgrim or gourd vases, having for subjects 'The Potter at His Wheel', 'The Oven for Burning the Clay', 'The Painting of the Ware', two tall square vases representing 'The Mining of the Cobalt', 'The Mixing of the Clay' and two vases of flat shape, 'The Making of Saggers' and 'The Enamel Kilns'. All these are very pretty and novel—but in this material we prefer a pair of large tusk-vases, elaborately pierced and carved and mounted on bronze stands, enriched with gilt birds and tortoises. In these the imitation is so admirable, that even on close inspection it is almost impossible to discover they are not remarkable specimens of dainty chiselling, for it is only by the touch detection is possible . . . We must note two exquisite figures by Hadley, of a Japanese lady and gentleman, remarkable alike for modelling and decoration."

In every style the modelling of James Hadley was indispensable, and the *Worcester Works Museum Catalogue* (1882) contains references to many examples ascribed to him, such as "Vase, in ivory porcelain, elephant head handles, decorated in bronze and gold, designed and modelled by Hadley". Perhaps his *tour de force* was a pair of large vases, shown at the 1878 Paris Exhibition. These vases were described by George Augustus Sala (*Paris Herself Again*, 1879): ". . . unquestionably the most important objects displayed by the famous Worcester establishment are the pair of large vases in the Renaissance style, ornamented with delicately modelled bas-reliefs in richly framed compartments on their sides. The subjects on one vase comprise the medieval potter working at his wheel and the modeller applying the finishing touches to the statuette of some saint, while represented on the other are the painter engaged on the decoration of a vase, and the furnace-man intent upon his anxious task. Admirably moulded heads of celebrated artists of the period of the Renaissance, who lent the aid of their great talents towards the production of the ceramic masterpieces of the epoch, form the handles . . ." Replicas of these vases were made and are preserved in the Works Museum (Plate 60).

Of James Hadley's more homely figure modelling, mention must be made of a charming series of children dressed in Kate Greenaway style costume. These figures, often with baskets for use on the table, are most attractive and were produced in large numbers over many years (Plate 62). These and other styles of Royal Worcester were often decorated in an expensive technique involving the use of variously tinted gold and other metallic colours.

For a short period in the 1870's the Worcester factory was experimenting in the production of figures and busts made in a terra-cotta body with turquoise blue enrichments. Of the later productions perhaps the best known are the delicately pierced or "reticulated" pieces made by George Owen. A contemporary account relates that "the artist tooled every one of these minute apertures without having any tracery, or any other assistance whatever to guide him to regularity, except his eye and his hand. . . . If on the last day of his work his knife had slipped, and so made two 'holes' into one, the whole piece would have been ruined" (*Pottery Gazette*, 1896). A photograph is here reproduced showing Owen at work on his incredibly thin walled masterpieces (Plate 65). George Owen's work is usually signed. Similar pierced objects were produced by semi-mechanical means over a long period.

GRAINGER COMPANY

Throughout the nineteenth century there was another factory in Worcester—the Grainger factory. In 1800 Thomas Grainger established his works in St. Martin's Street and in 1812 the firm became known as Grainger, Lee & Co. Good artists were employed and the large proportion of the wares that were made expressly for the London retailer, John Mortlock, bore Mortlock's name rather than the name of the factory. On the death of Thomas Grainger in 1839, his son George succeeded to the works, a fact recorded in the new factory mark of "G. Grainger & Co." in various forms. Up to the time of the 1851 Exhibition, the Grainger products followed closely the styles popular at the Chamberlain factory and "Japan" patterns formed an important part of the products.

In 1851 a new earthenware body, named "semi-porcelain" was introduced. This had, if all the qualities claimed for it are correct, remarkable utilitarian value. The Grainger company also produced a lot of parian, both in useful wares and in decorative figures and busts. Reticulated decoration appeared among the Grainger wares at the 1862 Exhibition. This pierced ware, originated by Chamberlains in 1845, was produced by the Grainger factory from the 1850's up to the opening years of the twentieth century, but the results are coarse in comparison with George Owen's masterpieces produced for the Royal Worcester company. *Pâte-sur-pâte* decoration was also used in the 1880's (Plate 85), but generally the Grainger wares followed closely the styles favoured at the Royal Worcester factory. In 1889 the Grainger company was incorporated with the larger Royal Worcester Porcelain company, but continued in production and used its former marks until 1902 when the Grainger works were finally closed.

LOCKE & COMPANY

Two Worcester factory hands established small independent factories in Worcester during the final years of the nineteenth century. In 1895 Edward Locke (b. 1829, d. 1909) established the Shrub Hill Works, helped by his large family of eleven, many of whom, like Edward, had been trained at the Royal Worcester factory or at Graingers. His products were mainly decorated with floral painting, and followed closely the Royal Worcester style. The *Pottery Gazette* of 1899 contains these comments: "In addition to the most costly art pieces which they pride themselves most upon, Messrs. Locke & Co. are producing a very large assortment of fancy goods at very moderate prices." This small factory was closed soon

56. The 'Norman Conquest' ewer and stand, one of the principal works completed by Thomas Bott for the Royal Worcester Company before his death in 1870. Shown at the 1871 Exhibition. Diameter of stand 12 in. Height of ewer 11½ in.

57
ROYAL WORCESTER.
'Norman Conquest'
vase (one of a pair)
painted by Thomas Bott
in his 'Limoges' style.
1871 and 1873
Exhibitions. Ht. 21 in.
Worcester Works Museum.

58
ROYAL WORCESTER vase
modelled in the Japanese
style by James Hadley.
c. 1877. Ht. 15 in.
Worcester Works Museum.

Page 130

59. ROYAL WORCESTER vase in the Japanese style. Designed by James Hadley. 1872 Exhibition. Ht. 10¼ in. Mark No. 55. *Victoria & Albert Museum.*

60. ROYAL WORCESTER. The 'Potter' vase (one of a pair) modelled by James Hadley, ornamented by Thomas and James Callowhill. 1878 Exhibition. Ht. 28 in. Mark No. 56. *Worcester Works Museum.*

Page 132

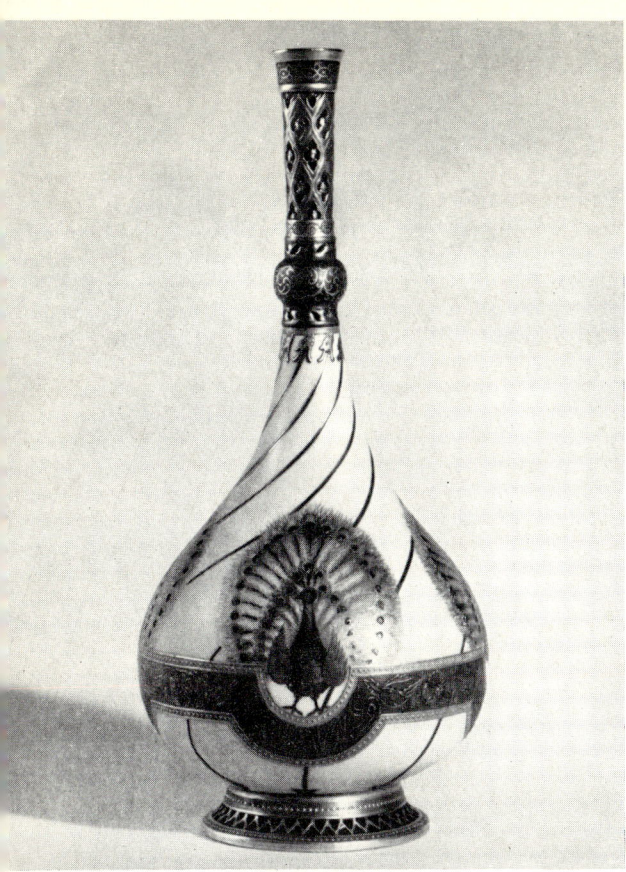

61

ROYAL WORCESTER vase, gilt in the Persian style. 1883 (Factory date mark). Ht. 12¼ in. Mark No. 56.

62

ROYAL WORCESTER. Three figures modelled by James Hadley in the 'Kate Greenaway' style. c. 1880–90. Mark No. 56

63
ROYAL WORCESTER
'Ivory' body nef modelled in the Italian style by James Hadley.
c. 1885. Ht. 15½ in. Mark No. 56.
Worcester Works Museum.

64
ROYAL WORCESTER
vase in the Louis XVI style, finely gilt.
c. 1889. Ht. 18 in.
Worcester Works Museum.

Page 134

65. MR. GEORGE OWEN at work on his intricately carved ROYAL WORCESTER vases etc.

66. A Chamberlain Worcester dish, decorated by GEORGE SPARKS with view of Whitley Court. *c.* 1845. Length 12½ in. Mark No. 68.

67
Typical HADLEY vase showing monochrome floral studies and coloured clay ornamentation at foot and neck. *c.* 1898. Ht. 12 in. Mark No. 66.

68
GRAINGER WORCESTER vase and cover painted by John Stinton. *c.* 1900. Ht. 15 in. Mark No. 62.

Page 136

after 1904, mainly because Locke lost a law action with the Royal Worcester company over the use of the word "Worcester" to describe his products.

HADLEY WARE

The Royal Worcester modeller James Hadley established himself in 1875 as an independent designer and modeller, but until 1894 his entire output was absorbed by the Royal Worcester company. In 1896, with the help of his three sons, he began manufacturing on his own account. His products were termed "Hadley Ware" and mainly comprised decorative vases with coloured clay enrichments and painted with floral compositions. Many of these are of high quality and are often painted in monochrome (Plate 67). The marks used by James Hadley are included with those of the other Worcester manufacturers in the Mark section, page 144. James Hadley died in December 1903 and, in July 1905, the business was taken over by the Royal Worcester company who continued to market wares in the Hadley tradition, under the direction of Louis Hadley.

An interesting first-hand account of the Hadley works and its productions is contained in the *Magazine of Art* for October 1898:

> I have had the honour of being the first visitor to a little manufactory of pottery where, unknown to the general public, very notable results indeed are being obtained. I was told that a pretty piece of ware which I saw in a friend's house at Worcester was not a new invention of the Royal Porcelain Works, but the work of an artist who, while remaining upon terms of perfect friendliness with the Royal Porcelain Works, on behalf of which he had worked for many years, had also been experimenting afresh on his own account and had at last achieved success. . . In his pleasant studio in the High Street at Worcester, and at his new works just built at Diglis you may see his beautiful process carried through from the modelling of the forms to the final burnishing of the completed work of art. Two years ago not a single piece of pottery had been made, though in view of the important step of not only designing but also making decorative pottery from first to last entirely by themselves, Mr. Hadley and his three sons were busy accumulating models some months earlier. Today (October 1898) may be seen a

complete little manufactory with two large kilns, painting room, electric polishing lathe, and grinding machinery complete. . . .

Take a large dish with raised scroll ornament in coloured clay on a white ground as an example of the method of "making". Into the "intaglio" hollows of the mould, which, of course, produces a counterpart in relief, the watery blue clay of the ornament is first carefully painted. . . . Then when the hollows are full to the brim, the edges being kept carefully cleaned of superfluous blue clay, after a short interval of partial drying, the white ground of the dish is laid over-all. The two different clays adhere, superfluous moisture sinks into the porous plaster of the mould, and after a time there emerges a dish with raised ornament for the firing. This is no mere dull earthenware production with only a surface glaze of colour, but a work of art in which body and ornament alike are formed of clays each of a uniform and homogeneous "through-colour". It will be seen at once that the body of this ware, or "faience" as Mr. Hadley names it, is an absolute novelty and superior in colour and texture to that of any former earthenware.

It will be seen that the ware of Mr. Hadley and his three sons, each of whom has a complete knowledge and direction of his special branch, shows nothing of the amateurism often characteristic of new ventures. It has found its way to appreciation without advertisement of any kind. Very few people have seen the examples in the tiny showroom in Worcester High Street, but their inherent merits of design and modelling, and originality of colour and material, have already opened up in the short space of a year and a half the prospect of a successful future.

Some confusion may be caused by the activities of independent decorators who practised in Worcester during the first half of the nineteenth century. George Sparks (b. 1804, d. 1874) was in Worcester from 1836 to 1854. He decorated Chamberlain and Coalport porcelain on his own account, a favourite subject being Witley Court; such inscriptions as "Witley Court, The Temporary Residence of Her Majesty Queen Adelaide and the Property of the Rt. Honle. Lord Ward" that occur on a fine tray (Plate 66) in the author's collection, date the examples to the period 1842 to 1846, at which time Queen Adelaide was living at Witley Court. The normal mark is "Sparks Worcester" written in red; on some specimens the inscription "By Appointment to Her Majesty Queen Adelaide" is added. George Sparks was later London agent for the Royal Worcester Company and for the Coalport Company. Two other Worcester painters, Enoch Doe and George Rogers, also decorated porcelain on their own account and their work is normally signed.

WORCESTER CERAMIC ARTISTS
(*Victorian Period only*)

* Artist given fuller mention in the text.

BAKER. Floral artist, Kerr & Binns period. 1852–62.

BALDWYN, C. H. C. Bird subjects, swans, etc., *c.* 1890 to *c.* 1904.

BATES, DAVID. Floral artist, *c.* 1860–80.

BEJOT, E. Gilder, designs in chased gold, etc., *c.* 1870–80.

BINNS, ALBERT. Son of R. W. Binns, rare experimental work, *c.* 1880, d. 1882.

*BOTT, THOMAS. Born 1829. Famous for his enamel painting, d. 1870.

BOTT, THOMAS JOHN. Born 1854, employed *c.* 1870–85, later Brown-Westhead, Moore and Coalport, d. 1932.

BRADLEY, JAMES. Animal, portrait and floral artist, *c.* 1852–60. (Father and son of the same name employed.)

BRECKNELL, JOSEPH. Designer and decorator, Chamberlains and Kerr & Binns.

BROCK, THOMAS (R.A.). Born 1847. Modeller at Worcester, *c.* 1860, d. 1922.

CALLOWHILL, JAMES. Figure subjects, heads, chased gilding, etc., *c.* 1855–85.

CALLOWHILL, THOMAS SCOTT. Figure subjects, heads, enamels, chased gilding, etc., *c.* 1855–85.

CHIVERS, F. H. Fruit painter, late nineteenth century. Later worked for Coalport.

COPSON, OCTAR H. Fruit painter, *c.* 1880.

CROOK, JAMES. Gilt decorative motifs, *c.* 1885.

DAVIS, HARRY. From 1898 into twentieth century.

DAVIS, JOSIAH. Born 1839. Fine gilder and designer, d. 1913. Employed *c.* 1855 onwards.

DOE, ENOCH, SENR. Scenic and figure painter. Chamberlains and earlier.

Doe, Enoch, Junr. Scenic and figure painter. Chamberlains and Kerr & Binns period.

Evans, David. Floral artist, early Grainger (also Copelands).

Evans, George. Modeller, c. 1870-1910.

*Hadley, James. Born c. 1837. Modeller. After 1875 worked on his own account, d. 1903.

Hopewell, John. Bird subjects, c. 1855-90

Kirk, W. B. Born 1824. Sculptor, modeller. Kerr & Binns, period 1852-62, d. 1900.

Lawton, S. Enamel and gilt decorations. Kerr & Binns period.

*Locke, Edward. Born 1829. Floral compositions. Later on his own account, d. 1909.

*Owen, George. Designer of openwork cut patterns. Late nineteenth century, early twentieth century, d. 1917.

Palmere, Charles. Figure subjects, etc., c. 1870-80.

Perling, Robert F. Landscape subjects, c. 1855-85.

Phillips, E. Floral artist, c. 1890-1932.

Powell, Walter. Hadley artist, c. 1900.

Powell, William. British birds, c. 1890-1950.

Raby, Edward. Floral artist, c. 1870-92. Later at Doultons.

Ranford, Samuel. Gilder and designer, c. 1855-90.

Rushton, Josiah. Figure painter, c. 1852-71.

Salter, Edward. Landscape and English cattle, c. 1895-1902.

Sherriff, James (Senr. and Junr.) Senr. Floral artist, Kerr & Binns period. Junr. Butterflies, etc., c. 1880.

Stinton, John. Born 1854. Landscapes, cattle, etc. Originally with Graingers. Late nineteenth, early twentieth century, d. 1956.

Sutton, F. Figure subjects, c. 1880.

Taylor, William. Floral painter, c. 1845-55.

Toft, Charles. Born 1831. Kerr & Binns modeller, parian busts, etc. Later at Mintons and Wedgwoods, d. 1909.

Weaver, James. Bird painter, c. 1853-70. Subsequently at Copelands.

Wells, Luke. Animal subjects, etc., c. 1852-65. (Father and son employed.)

Williams, Joseph. Animal subjects, scenic, etc., c. 1860-75.

WORCESTER MARKS

Mark No.

CHAMBERLAIN & CO.
WORCESTER
155, NEW BOND ST,
& NO 1.
COVENTRY ST.
LONDON.

47 Printed Chamberlain mark, *c.* 1840–45. Similar marks without the Coventry Street address are pre-Victorian.

Chamberlain & Co.
Worcester.

48 Printed or written mark, *c.* 1847.

CHAMBERLAINS

49 Impressed and printed mark, *c.* 1847–50.

50 Printed mark. *c.* 1850–52. (A similar mark bearing the words "Royal Porcelain Works" was used by Kerr & Binns, *c.* 1852–6.)

51 Kerr & Binns printed or impressed mark without crown. 1852–62.

52 Rare Kerr & Binns period printed mark, *c.* 1856, occurring on Parian group, Plate 77.

53 Kerr & Binns printed shield mark used on the finest pieces, incorporating the last two numbers of the year (often indistinct) and in this case Thomas Bott's initials, T. B., *c.* 1854–62.

VICTORIAN PORCELAIN

Mark No.

54 Printed or impressed, *c.* 1862–70, rarely used.

Some transitional Kerr & Binns—Royal Worcester pieces are marked with the printed crown placed above the impressed Kerr & Binns circular mark. Such pieces were potted in the Kerr & Binns period but decorated later.

Mark No.

55 "Royal Worcester" mark (printed or impressed). Note crown added to Kerr & Binns mark—1862 onwards. Figure occurring under mark indicates year, i.e. 1873.

56 From 1867 year letters were placed under the standard factory mark. This system ceased in 1890.
See Table B, page 145.

57 From 1891 "Royal Worcester. England" was added to the standard mark. A system of dating by means of dots was also introduced.
11 = 1902.
See Table B, page 145.

Other marks were occasionally used all incorporating the words "Worcester Royal Porcelain Works".

Mark No.

58 Rare printed mark used to denote an experimental body, *c.* 1896.

WORCESTER 143

Mark No.

Grainger Lee & Co. Worcester. 59 Written or printed mark, *c.* 1812+.

George Grainger. Royal China Works. Worcester. 60 Written mark, *c.* 1840+. Other marks occur, incorporating the title "G. Grainger". George Grainger succeeded his father in 1839.

61 Printed or impressed Grainger shield mark, *c.* 1870+.
Other marks incorporating the initials G G & Co, G & Co W. occur.

62 Later printed Grainger mark. "Royal China Works. Worcester" added *c.* 1889.
"England" added *c.* 1891.
Note that mark No. 62 has a letter (H) below the main mark. As different letters occur it may be presumed that a dating system was employed similar to that of the Royal Worcester Company.
The following table has been drawn up, based on a single dated example, bearing the year letter "L". At the time of writing it has not proved possible to check other letters due to the absence of dated examples and therefore the table can only be regarded as provisional. It is hoped in publishing this provisional table that information may be forthcoming that will

Mark
No.
62   help to establish the accuracy of
contd.   these dates:

A 1891	F 1896	K 1901
B 1892	G 1897	L 1902
C 1893	H 1898	M 1903
D 1894	I 1899	N 1904
E 1895	J 1900	

63   Printed marks of Locke & Co late nineteenth century, c. 1895+.

64   c. 1900–04

65   Hadley mark, printed or impressed, c. 1896 to February 1897.

66   Printed "Hadley's Faience" mark, used from February 1897 to June 1900. Similar mark without "Faience" used from June 1900 to August 1902.

67   Hadley mark, August 1902 to June 30th, 1905.

68   Written mark of the independent decorator, George Sparks, c. 1842+.

TABLE B

KEY TO DATES OF ROYAL WORCESTER MANUFACTURE FROM 1867–1915

The key letters set out below correspond to the year of manufacture. They were printed below the factory mark. The example on the right represents the year 1890.

A	1867	K	1875	U	1883
B	1868	L	1876	V	1884
C	1869	M	1877	W	1885
D	1870	N	1878	X	1886
E	1871	P	1879	Y	1887
G	1872	R	1880	Z	1888
H	1873	S	1881	O	1889
I	1874	T	1882	a	1890

No code letter was used in 1891 but the words "Royal Worcester England" were added in the form of a wreath round the main symbol. Successive years were indicated by a system of dots placed between the surrounding lettering and the surmounting crown—one dot for each year. Thus 1892 was indicated by a single dot placed over the R. of "Royal"; 1893 by a dot over the R of "Royal" and one over the D of "England". This went on until 1915 when there were twenty-four dots in all.

The accompanying example shows the standard mark with eleven dots added. It therefore represents the year 1902.

ROYAL WORCESTER PATTERN NUMBERS

A simple progressive unprefixed system of pattern numbering was employed during the 1860's and the greater part of the 1870's. This system was terminated at 9699 about 1878.

A new series was then started bearing the prefix "B". This was of short duration, terminating at B1080 in 1880.

For the remainder of the Victorian era a prefix letter W was used.

By 1900 the pattern numbers had reached W5793—at this date the ornamental model number (mainly found impressed on vases and figures) had reached 2101.

It should be borne in mind that the date numbers, letters and cyphers found on marked specimens give a more accurate means of dating. Any list of pattern numbers can only indicate the date when the pattern was first introduced, not the date of production.

As with other factories, the unrepetitive work of the foremost artists do not bear pattern numbers although, with vases, the shape or model number may occur.

CHAMBERLAIN OPENWORK FOOTED BOWL. 1846.

CHAPTER 7

THE PARIAN BODY

WHITE parian, or statuary porcelain as it was originally called, was a great favourite with the Victorian manufacturers, not only on account of its decorative merits but also because its composition made it highly suitable for moulding in intricate forms.

Experiments had undoubtedly been made, and various dry unglazed bodies introduced, during the 1820's and 30's; but these bodies were of the nature of stoneware rather than porcelain, and they were chiefly used for such wares as moulded jugs with raised motifs and for small floral encrusted articles.

An unsubstantiated account of the introduction of the parian body in 1842 is contained in R. Hunt's *Hand-book to the Official Catalogues of the Great Exhibition* published in 1851: "The first idea of imitating marble in ceramic manufacture originated with Mr. Thomas Battam, the artist directing the extensive porcelain manufactory of Mr. Alderman Copeland at Stoke-upon-Trent, in the commencement of 1842. After a series of experiments he succeeded in producing a very perfect imitation of marble, both in surface and tint. One of the earliest specimens was submitted to His Grace the Duke of Sutherland, who expressed his unqualified admiration of the purposes to which it was applied, and became its first patron by purchasing the example submitted. This was on the 3rd. of August 1842. . . ." It must be remembered however that Hunt is not regarded as a very reliable source and that no mention is to be found in contemporary journals of the production of Copelands' statuary porcelain or parian at the period claimed by Hunt for its introduction.

The first contemporary notice of statuary porcelain or parian is contained in the January 1845 issue of the *Art Union* magazine and is contained in a report of the Art-Union of London: ". . . This brings us to one of the most recent, and, as we will venture to predict, one of the most popular acts of the Committee. . . . The Committee have constantly adverted in their reports to the connexion between Manufacturers and Art, and have felt the importance of bringing one to the aid of the other. As a first step, they have determined to reduce some fine statue to a convenient size, and to issue a certain number of copies in stone china, as manufactured by Messrs. Copeland & Garrett. Mr. Gibson, our eminent countryman, has offered any of his works for this purpose, and we have little doubt that an impetus will thus be given which will be felt throughout the whole of the Potteries and lead to much good. . . ."

An interesting footnote mentions two early examples which had been seen by the magazine's representative: ". . . We have been enabled to examine the material referred to, and can bear testimony to its beauty, as well as very valuable qualities for multiplying the sculptor's work. . . . Messrs. Copeland & Garrett have already produced some beautiful examples in the material, one a statue of a Shepherd Boy by Wyatt (lent to them for the purpose by the Duke of Sutherland), and one, a copy of Marochetti's famous equestrian statue of Philibert." It will thus be seen that Copeland & Garrett were producing parian figures in 1844.

Some fifteen years later the *Art Journal* (the new title of *The Art Union* magazine from 1849) contains a further interesting account describing how this magazine introduced the new ware to the Art-Union of London: "When we visited the works of Mr. Alderman Copeland—then 'Copeland & Garrett' at Stoke-on-Trent, we there witnessed the first efforts to secure popularity for the new art of Porcelain sculpture. Two statuettes had been produced in it, one a graceful female bust, and the other 'the Shepherd Boy' after Wyatt, but they had not 'Sold'. The public did not show any sign of being prepared to acknowledge the real worthiness of the novelty; and it is by no means improbable that the process would have proceeded no further, had it not been our good fortune to urge upon Mr. Garrett the wisdom of perseverance . . . a meeting was, in consequence, arranged by us between several sculptors, of whom Mr. Gibson was one, and Mr. T. Battam, the artist of the works. The two honorary secretaries of the Art-Union of London were also present. After a careful examination of the new material an opinion was pronounced decidedly in its favour. Mr. Gibson declaring it to be 'the material next best to marble that he had ever seen' and his brothers in Art agreeing with him. A commission from the Art-Union of London followed, and this new art of parian sculpture was rescued from a peril that might have proved fatal in the first infancy of its career."

The first work commissioned by the Art-Union of London in the parian body was Gibson's "The Narcissus" (Plate 69). The Committee's report as submitted to the Annual Meeting on April 22nd, 1845, contains the following passage: "Your Committee have long borne in view the connexion between Manufacturers and Art, and have felt the importance of leading one to the aid of the other. Considering the porcelain manufacture to be of considerable consequence, and greatly dependent on Art, they propose to reduce a statue of convenient size, and to issue a certain number of copies in that material. Mr. Gibson, R.A., when in England, kindly offered the use of any of his works for this purpose, and the Committee have determined on adapting 'The Narcissus' for the first experiment, his diploma piece at the Royal Academy. Some difficulties which arose at the Royal Academy have delayed the completion of the intention, but these are now removed, and the work will be proceeded with immediately by Messrs. Copeland & Garrett."

The figure of the Narcissus was duly completed and early in 1846 fifty copies were given as prizes. It is interesting to note that the cost of these statuettes is given in the Art-Union's published accounts as one hundred and fifty pounds or three pounds per figure. In the November issue of the magazine *Art Union* we learn that the first commission met with favour and that a further statuette was ordered for the following year. "Those already finished are extremely beautiful and so satisfactory that a further commission from the Society has resulted ... the Committee of the Art-Union of London having awarded to Mr. Foley one hundred guineas for a reduced copy of his beautiful statue of 'Innocence' also to be executed in Statuary porcelain." So successful were these first two models that they were included in the prize lists for many years. Having seen the influence that the Art-Union of London had in the successful development of the parian body, it might now be appropriate to explain some of the background of this, and many similar societies.

The Art-Union of London was formed in 1836. In return for an annual subscription each member was entitled to participate in an annual draw, the top prizes being works of art (chiefly paintings from the Royal Academy Exhibitions) valued at some hundreds of pounds each. It was obvious that the reproductions of famous sculptured figures and groups in the new statuary porcelain, being easy and inexpensive to produce in quantity, were ideal for many of the numerous lesser prizes that were also drawn. Moreover these figures had, at the period, a high novelty and decorative value and made a welcome change from the medals, lithographs and engravings that had previously been awarded.

The Art-Union movement gained in popularity and was legalised by Act of Parliament in 1846 having previously contravened the laws relating to lotteries. Various smaller Art-Unions were formed and from the ceramic point of view, the most notable of these was the Crystal Palace Art-Union which began in 1858 and was renamed, in 1865, The Ceramic and Crystal Palace Art-Union. The Royal Irish Art-Union also commissioned many works in parian and other ceramic bodies. Prince Albert gave the Unions every encouragement "feeling assured that these institutions will exercise a most beneficial influence on the Arts" (*Art Journal*). Many special works were commissioned by the Unions which, at the peak of their popularity, had considerable sums of money at their disposal. While they commissioned many works in parian, "Majolica", porcelain and pottery and so helped to bring well-designed ceramics into the homes of people who were perhaps otherwise disinterested, it should be borne in mind that their main object was to sell, by means of lottery, large pieces of sculpture, oil paintings and water colours. All Art-Union prizes in the ceramic field are distinctly marked and were exclusively intended for distribution as prizes by the Union concerned.

Apart from the evidence of the early Art-Union commissions, we have an account of statuary porcelain being included in the Copeland stand at the Manchester "Exposition of British Industrial Art". This review, published in the *Art Union* of January 1846, is illustrated with an engraving of the stand (page 21) showing, among other items, the equestrian statue of Emmanuel Philibert and The Shepherd Boy, both of which had been mentioned a year earlier. The review also mentions other early statuettes and, by including a notice of a large vase in parian, shows that the possibilities of this new body were being quickly exploited. "Of statuettes there are many examples ... of a character wholly distinct from the class generally known as bisque or pottery figures. ... We direct particular attention to a copy of Marochetti's statue of 'Philibert'. ... Of other statuettes, the visitor will not fail to be delighted with those of Fiamingo. It is impossible to devise more apt or desirable ornaments for the drawing room; far from being costly like bronze or marble, they are infinitely more pure and beautiful than plaster, occupying indeed a place between the two. Of the Statuary vases we give two engravings. The vase is thirty inches in height, copied from a marble vase in the British Museum, with a slight alteration in the neck to adapt it for use as a flower vase." The works mentioned in this account which is dated January 1846, must have been produced in 1845 or earlier.

While it is now generally agreed that Copelands were the first manufacturers to introduce this body on a commercial scale, it must be remembered that Thomas Boote of T. & R. Boote (Burslem) claimed to have introduced the body as early as 1841. Reference has already been made to the use of various unglazed bodies for useful wares, and Minton's sketch books for the period 1831–42 include "parian" articles. Copelands were no doubt first to introduce and use the new body in imitation of marble for the production of figures and groups, but there is some doubt as to who actually invented it. The *Art Union* magazine gives the credit to Thomas Battam, Copelands' Art Director, with such statements as: "It is but justice to Mr. Battam, the artistic director of Messrs. Copeland's establishment, to state that the original idea and introduction of this material is wholly attributable to his taste and judgement." Elsewhere in the same journal the credit is given to Spencer Garrett of Copeland & Garrett. It is probable that the honour should really be given to a former Derby workman employed by Copeland & Garrett—John Mountford—who is not mentioned in the *Art Union* magazine. Mountford was trying to imitate the beautiful early Derby white bisque body that had been employed in the production of the graceful eighteenth-century Derby figures and groups. His former employer, Sampson Hancock of Derby, related to a *Pottery Gazette* reporter in 1895: "He (Mountford) was apprenticed at the old works in Derby, but left early in life, and came to Messrs. Copeland & Garrett's at Stoke-on-Trent to start the figure trade there. While in their employ, he brought out the composition known to the trade as parian . . . the name of this man will be recorded in time to come among those of famous potters." But in point of fact, it was Battam and Garrett who received most of the publicity. John Haslem, in his *The Old Derby China Factory*, published in 1876, acknowledges that Mountford actually discovered the new body but adds that: "It is not unlikely that Battam would see the value of the new body, and the use to be made of it sooner than Mountford and he might therefore have been instrumental in its first introduction."

Although most of the contemporary journals referred to the new body as statuary porcelain, the manufacturers marketed it under different names; but, in each case, the name used emphasised the strong similarity that the material bore to marble. Copelands originated and continued to use the term statuary porcelain, but Mintons and Wedgwoods respectively used the names parian and Carrara.

The marble-like qualities of the material were underlined in almost every contemporary review. "The object attempted has been to present as close an approximation to marble as the various articles available to the manufacture could realise—statuary porcelain, as this new form of material is called, is scarcely inferior to marble as a material for art. We may therefore fairly regard its introduction as one of the greatest additions to the bounds of artistic production which we have had to record for many a long year" (*Art Union*, 1847).

The method used by Copelands for the manufacture of parian has been ably described by Thomas Battam, then Art Director, writing in 1849:

> The material is used in a liquid state, technically termed "slip" about the consistency of thick cream. It is poured into the moulds forming the figure or group, which, being made of plaster, rapidly absorb a portion of the moisture, and the coating immediately next to the mould soon becomes of a sufficient thickness for the cast, when the superfluous "slip" is poured back. The cast remains in the moulds for some time at a high temperature, by which it is (through the evaporation that has taken place), reduced to a state of clay, and is sufficiently firm to bear its own weight when released from the moulds, which are then opened, and the different portions of the subject taken out.
>
> Each figure requires many moulds—the head, arms and hands, legs, body parts of the drapery, when introduced, and the other details of the subject are generally moulded separately. In one group, representing "The Return from the Vintage" consisting of seven figures, there are upwards of fifty moulds, and, each of these in several dimensions; these parts being removed, have then to be repaired, the seams caused by the junctions of the mould cleaned off and the whole put together. This is a process requiring, when well executed, the greatest nicety and judgement,

69. COPELAND parian figure 'Narcissus' by John Gibson, R.A. The first figure commissioned by the Art Union of London in 1846. Ht. 11⅞ in. *Victoria & Albert Museum.*

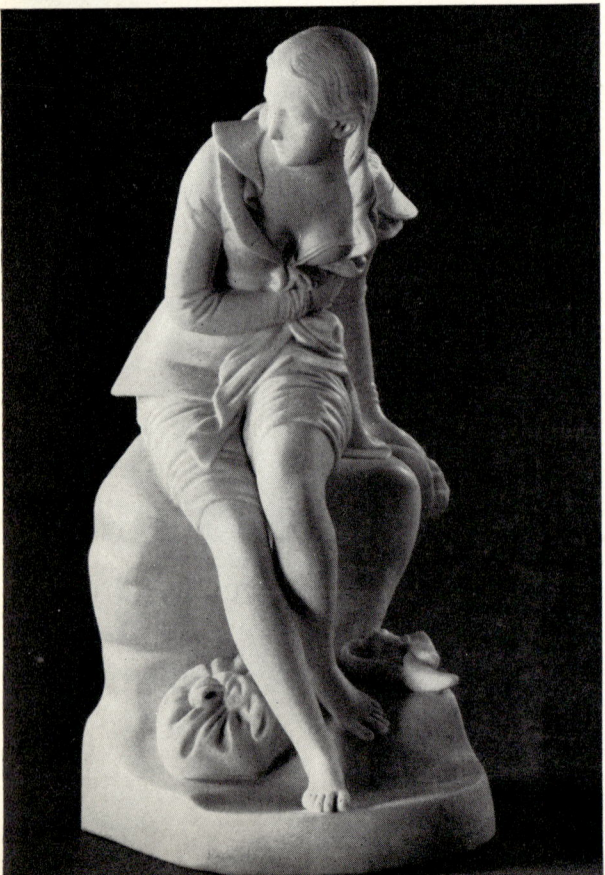

70
MINTON parian group 'Una and the Lion' by John Bell, made for Summerly's Art Manufactures in 1847. Ht. 14 in. Mark No. 35.

71
MINTON parian figure 'Dorothea' by John Bell, made for Summerly's Art Manufactures in 1847. Ht. 13¼ in. Mark No. 35.

Page 154

72. MINTON parian figure 'Mercury'. *c.* 1850. Ht. 15¼ in. *Victoria & Albert Museum.*

Page 155

73
MINTON parian figure 'Miranda' by John Bell. *c.* 1850. Ht. 14½ in.

74
MINTON parian group 'Naomi and her daughters-in-law.' *c.* 1850. Ht. 13 in.

Page 156

75. MINTON parian and glazed porcelain covered bowl. A duplicate from a service shown at the 1851 Exhibition and presented by Queen Victoria to the Emperor of Austria. Ht. 10 in. *Victoria & Albert Museum.*

76
Copelands' 'Ino and Bacchus', from the original by J. H. Foley. Originally shown at the 1851 Exhibition. Length 20 in.

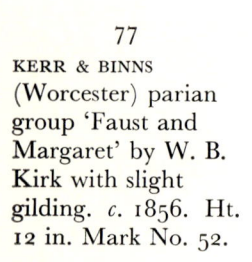

77
KERR & BINNS (Worcester) parian group 'Faust and Margaret' by W. B. Kirk with slight gilding. *c.* 1856. Ht. 12 in. Mark No. 52.

Page 158

78
Parian group made by
W. ADAMS & SONS.
c. 1860. Ht. 12½ in.

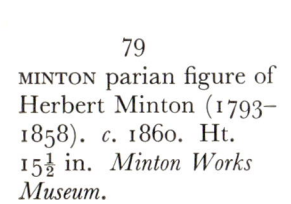

79
MINTON parian figure of Herbert Minton (1793–1858). c. 1860. Ht. 15½ in. *Minton Works Museum.*

Page 159

80. Three small brooches in parian. *c.* 1860.

the fragile nature of the material in its present state rendering considerable practical knowledge necessary to form a perfect union of the different members. . . .

Peculiar care is required in putting together nude figures, in which the junction of the parts generally presenting a level circular surface, requires the decision of an educated eye to fix with accuracy. . . . Want of judgement in this respect will often cause such a deviation of outline, as seriously to injure the beauty of the work. The parts are attached together by a "slip", similar to that used for casting; the surfaces to be joined together being either dipped into them, or the "slip" is applied with a pencil, and, according to the discretion with which this is executed, and the neatness with which the sections of the moulds are made to fit, will be the greater or less prominence of the seams which so often disfigure pottery castings . . . The "slip" in this case is merely required to soften the surface of the clay of the members which have to be united, just sufficiently to cause adhesion. All that is used beyond that requirement is not only superfluous but actually detrimental; moistening the parts to which it is applied so much that the edges become pliant, and yielding to the pressure while being attached, distort the outline, and by causing unequal shrinking in the process of firing the junctures become evident and unsightly. . . .

The figure or group being thus put together remains two or three days. When being sufficiently dry, it is supported by "props" made of the same material placed in such a position as to bear a portion of the weight and prevent any undue pressure that might cause the figure to sink or yield in the "firing". Each end of the "prop" is embedded in a coating of ground flint to prevent adhesion, and is thus easily removed. It is then placed in the oven and submitted to a heat of about 60° of Wedgwood's pyrometer (approx. 1100° C.). This operation, which is gradually effected, occupies from sixty to seventy hours. The fires are then withdrawn and the oven allowed to cool; and when sufficiently so, the figures are drawn out, the seams rubbed down; they are again placed in "Saggars" and embedded in sand and then refired at a still higher temperature than they were previously submitted to. . . . It is even sometimes necessary to fire casts three times, a peculiar degree of heat being required to produce the extreme beauty of surface which the finest specimens present.

The total contraction of the figures from the mould to the finished state is one-fourth. The contraction of the "slip" with which the mould is first charged, to the state in which it leaves the mould, is one-sixteenth; again it contracts another one-sixteenth in the process of drying for the oven and one-eighth in the process of vitrification, so that a model two feet high will produce a fired cast of eighteen inches only. Mr. Minton states the contraction of their improved composition as being but little more than one-fifth. . . . The chemical elements of this composition are essentially alumina, silica and felspar, which, by the action of the intense heat to which the mass is exposed, actually agglutinate so as to form the beautiful body which the finished figures present, the perfection of which is still more apparent in a fractured portion . . . (*Art Journal*, 1849).

Although no mention is made of the fact, the parian body generally received the slightest suspicion of a surface glaze.

It is from Léon Arnoux, Mintons' Art Director, that we learn how the soft characteristic colour of English parian was produced: "The firing itself requires great attention, for on the way it is managed depends the colour of the biscuit. This colour is not given by any material mixed in the compound, but by the small quantity of oxide of iron which is contained in the clays and felspar, pure as they may be. During the firing, as the atmosphere of the inside is oxidising, this small quantity of iron forms with the silica of peroxide of iron, which like all peroxidised salts of this metal, has a yellowish red colour. It is the small quantity of that salt spread in the mass which gives that yellowish white colour which is so agreeable. If, on the contrary, by neglect or any other reason, there should be a great amount of smoke or flame, the nature of the atmosphere changing the peroxide would be greatly reduced, and the result would be a salt of protoxide of iron, manifest by its bluish-green colour. In this last case, the parian loses the greatest part of its beauty . . ." (quoted in Chaffer's *Marks and Monograms*).

When figures and groups were taken from original large-size sculpture, the reduced scale model, from which the moulds were taken, was often produced by means of Benjamin Cheverton's reducing machine. This was a machine whereby an exact small-scale replica could be obtained of any statue or similar object. It had previously been used in reducing full-sized figures and busts to cabinet size; and it now proved invaluable to the firms making parian figures, since it saved the difficulties and uncertainties of producing by hand the first model on a scale suitable for production in parian. It is probable that Cheverton (b. 1794, d. 1876) first made the reduced figures in alabaster in his own studio and from these the manufacturers could then produce their master moulds. The inscription "Cheverton Sc." found on some parian pieces denotes that the example was reduced from an original work by the reducing machine.

There would seem to be nothing capable of manufacture in earthenware or porcelain that was not tried out also in parian, from life size statues (at Copelands) to shirt studs and delicately worked floral jewellery (Plate 80). A most attractive use of parian practised by Copeland, Coalport, Minton, Worcester and the Belleek factory in Ireland was in combining the matt parian with porcelain or with glazed parian (Plates 75 and 81). Figure-supported centrepieces or comports were most successful when carried out in this manner, and were introduced by Copelands as early as 1846: "A variety has just been produced as ornaments of the dessert table, in lieu of the usual compotiers . . . one service, in which the Seasons are introduced supporting the baskets, is beautiful both in conception and execution. The figures are in statuary, and the baskets enamelled in turquoise and gold . . ." (*Art Union*, 1846). These centrepieces with parian supports were at the height of their popularity by 1851. Many Copeland comports and baskets were originally fitted with coloured glass liners which not only contrasted pleasantly with the openwork basket design but also made the pieces capable of holding water.

Parian was also used in conjunction with other materials, and the most noteworthy of these composite effects were the Potts' metal and parian ornaments introduced in 1848 as a result of a suggestion published in the *Art Union* magazine: "We have on several occasions advised the union of statuary porcelain with metal, and it gives us much pleasure to see our suggestion very satisfactorily carried out by Mr. Potts, the eminent manufacturer of Birmingham. The objects he has hitherto produced on this plan consist of flower vases, candle lamps and gas brackets . . . the metal is of brass, bronze, or electro silvered or gilt, the figures are of Copelands statuary porcelain. . . . The figures, which are skilfully combined with the metal, are from models chiefly by Mr. Woolner, a young sculptor of great promise...." Similar wares were shown at the 1851 exhibition by R. W. Winfield of Birmingham and one of these pieces was bought by Queen Victoria for Osborne House.

Up to this point the story of parian has been chiefly concerned with the period before 1851 and with its development by Copelands. Naturally, once the body was successfully established, other manufacturers strove to produce similar wares; but few were successful before 1851.

At the 1851 Exhibition parian wares were exhibited only by Bell of Glasgow, T. & R. Boote, Coalport, Copeland, J. Edwards, Grainger (of Worcester), T. Hughes, Keys & Mountford, Charles Meigh, Minton and Wedgwood. Several of the early Minton models, from 1847 onwards were made for Summerly's Art Manufactures (see Chapter 9), and these examples (Plates 70 and 71) bear a raised medallion bearing the initials F.S. together with Minton's ermine mark and the name of the sculptor—John Bell (Mark No. 35). Mintons also used the parian body for some ornamental table wares, and all their later *pâte-sur-pâte* work was carried out on a tinted parian body. From 1850 onwards many figures were modelled by the French artists working for Mintons and other factories. In this connection such names as Emile Jeannest, Hugues Protat and Albert Carrier-Belleuse are of international repute.

During the second half of the nineteenth century, a multitude of factories, many of small size, flooded the market with thousands of parian figures of varying quality and design. As a general rule, these lesser manufacturers did not mark their wares and it can serve no useful purpose to list them, especially as a complete list would probably contain over one hundred names. The firm of Robinson & Leadbetter (established in 1850) must, however, be mentioned, as they devoted their whole production to work in the parian body; and they continued to use the material well into the twentieth century, long after it had been abandoned by most of the other manufacturers. They employed the celebrated young modeller Roland Morris. Most of Robinson & Leadbetter's wares are unmarked. Examples of their parian figures are sometimes coloured and gilt and similar in general appearance to many Continental wares. The initials "(R.L.)" occasionally occur impressed into the base, and "Ltd" occurs added to the marks after 1887.

Victorian parian figures and groups provide an opportunity for collectors who are looking for an inexpensive field in which to form

THE PARIAN BODY 165

a collection. While it would doubtless be impossible to trace every model made during the Victorian era, it might be interesting to collect pieces produced by any one factory or to confine one's attention to the various Art-Union prizes or to the work of an individual sculptor. To help in the formation of any such collection a list of the principal models produced up to the time of the 1851 Exhibition is given on pages 166–9.

COPELAND & GARRETT "STATUARY" VASE, 1846.

LIST OF THE PRINCIPAL PARIAN FIGURES AND GROUPS INTRODUCED PRIOR TO 1851

T. & R. Boote

Parian included in the 1851 Exhibition

    Bust of Sir Robert Peel.
    Shakespeare. Twenty inches high.
    Milton.
    Venus.
    Rustic group—The Mother.
    Large Allegorical group—Repentance, Faith & Resignation.

Coalport (John Rose & Co.)

    The Cornish Wife at the Well of St. Keyne, *c.* 1849.
    Bacchus & Ariadne, *c.* 1849.

Parian included in the 1851 Exhibition

    Group—The Pleiades adorning Night.
    Group—Puck & Companions.
    Clock case, figures of Time & Cupid.
    Pair of Wrestling figures.

Copeland

Models marked * were included in the 1851 Exhibition

  1844 Female bust.
      *The Shepherd Boy (Wyatt).
      *Equestrian figure of Philibert—Duke of Savoy (Marochetti).
  1845 *The Narcissus (Gibson). Art-Union of London, 1846.
      *Paul & Virginia—a group (Cumberworth).
      Psyche.
      Vase—nude children on rocky base. Twenty-four inches high.
  1846 Apollo (Wyatt).
      Shakespeare.
  1847 *Innocence (Foley). Art-Union of London, 1848.
      Bust of Flora.
      *Bust of Jenny Lind (Durham).

Ondine.
Eve.
Cupid chained.
1848 *The Four Royal Children as the Seasons (Mrs. Thornycroft).
1849 Bust of Her Majesty (Francis).
Bust of the Duke of Wellington (Count d'Orsay).
*Venus (Gibson).
*Sabrina (Marshall).
Last Drop (Marshall).
*Indian Fruit Girl & Water Bearer. A pair (Cumberworth).
*Ino & the Infant Bacchus (Foley). (*Plate 76*).
*Dancing Girl reposing (Marshall). Art-Union of London, 1850.
1849 *The Return from the Vintage.
1850 *Bust of Sir Robert Peel (Westmacott).
*Lady Godiva (Macbride).
*The Prodigal Son (Theed).
*Head of Juno.
*Duke of Sutherland (Francis).
1851 *Sappho (Theed).
*Rebecca (Theed).
*The Astragali Players.
*The Girl with Scorpion.
*Sir Walter Scott.
*Group of Graces.
*Group of Cupids.
*The Bride.
*The Sea Nymph.
*Lord George Bentinck.
*Lady Clementina Villiers.
*Princess Helena.
*The Portland Vase.

KEYS & MOUNTFORD

Parian included in the 1851 Exhibition

Flora.
Prometheus tormented by the vulture.
Two Circassian Slaves.
Venus unrobing at the Bath.

Venus extracting a Thorn.
Various figure supported comports, centrepieces, etc.

N.B. The partner Mountford was JOHN MOUNTFORD the originator of the parian body while employed at Copelands. He later separated from Keys and manufactured parian on his own account; his signature occurs on some specimens.

CHARLES MEIGH & SONS

Parian included in the 1851 Exhibition

Templar & Companion.
Falconer & Companion.
Bather & Companion.
Cupid & Venus.
Dancer & Companion.
Flora.
Prometheus.
Clock Case—Night & Morning.

MINTONS

*Models marked * were included in the 1851 Exhibition*

1847 *Ariadne on a Panther. ⎫ Exhibited at The Society of
    Mercury. ⎭ Arts, March 1847.
    *Una and the Lion (John Bell). Summerly's Art Manufactures (Plate 70).
    *Dorothea (John Bell). Summerly's Art Manufactures (Plate 71).
    St. Joseph.
    Ophelia.
    Cleopatra.
    Dancing Girl.
    Jenny Lind.
    Hebe.
    Kissing Cupids.
1848 Apollo.
    Magdalen.
    *Naomi and her daughters-in-law (Plate 74).
    *Shakespeare.
    Comedy & Tragedy.
    The Rose of England.
    The Crucifixion.

1849 *Temperance.
    *Babes in the Wood.
    Christ.
    *The Flight into Egypt.
    Sleeping Cupid.
    Dying Gladiator.
    The First Mother.
1850 *Miranda (Plate 73).
    *The Amazon.
    Bird Catcher.
    Coquette.
    Juvenile Contention.
    Raphael.
    Atala & Chactas.
    *Love Restraining Wrath.
    *Sir Robert Peel.
    *Theseus.
    *Venus & Astrid.
    *Flora.
    *Children with Goat (a pair).

Note: Due to the fact that the factory records are not dated the above lists may be slightly inaccurate. For instance, a figure listed under 1848 may not have been introduced until early in 1849. Many of the more popular models continued in production long after they were first introduced.

WEDGWOOD

Mentioned in the *Art Journal* of 1849
  Triton.
  Cupid & Psyche.
  Fawn.
  Infant Bacchus.
  Diana.

1851 Exhibition Models
  Venus & Cupid (twenty-seven inches high).
  Cupid (twenty-four inches high).
  Infant Hercules.
  Morpheus.
  Venus.
  Mercury.

CHAPTER 8

PÂTE-SUR-PÂTE

THE *pâte-sur-pâte* style of decoration provides one of the many instances where the Victorian potters in seeking to copy earlier wares (in this case Chinese) developed a style of decorating which was wholly nineteenth century in character. Some of the finest masterpieces of Victorian ceramic art were decorated by this painstaking technique in which thin washes of white "slip" were built up over a tinted ground resulting in a cameo-like effect.

We are fortunate in that the accepted master of this technique, M. L. Solon, wrote two accounts of his life and methods of work. The first was published in *Studio* of January 1894 and extracts from this are contained in an article by the present author printed in *The Connoisseur*, June 1954. Solon's second article appeared in the *Art Journal* for March 1901 and this is of the greatest interest as it gives the early history of *pâte-sur-pâte* together with a description of the process as practised by Solon at Mintons.

Marc Louis Solon was born at Montauban in 1835. After early training in Paris at the Atelier Lecoq he was employed at the French National Factory at Sèvres where he received the training that was to provide the basis for his later skill. While still in France he produced plaques in the *pâte-sur-pâte* style for the Paris art dealer, E. Rousseau. Examples of this period were normally signed "Miles". In 1870, on account of the unsettled conditions in France resulting from the Franco-Prussian war, Solon came to England and was immediately attracted to Mintons at Stoke where, he relates, the day after his arrival he was at work experimenting with the body and glazes used at the Minton factory.

Solon described his early experiments in France in his *Art Journal* article:

> One of the innovations from which arose the greatest expectations was the altogether new method of decorating the porcelain before any firing had taken place by the application of white reliefs upon coloured grounds: a process which received the

appropriate name of "*Pâte-sur-Pâte*", that is "body upon body". The first idea was derived from a Chinese vase preserved in the ceramic museum, which showed a design of flowers and foliage of white paste heavily embossed upon a celadon ground. Simple as the scheme may appear, various difficulties were experienced before it could be brought to complete realisation, the worst of these being that the perfect adherence of the applied parts could never be depended upon; they cracked, blistered, or fell off in the course of the firing. At last, the obstacle being overcome and the right way of proceeding having been definitely settled, it was found that the result arrived at went far beyond the end it had been intended to reach; in short, that the merit of the imitation far surpassed that of the model.

I was asked to try my hand at the new process, and two sculptors, who were then practising it with success, initiated me—I cannot say with an evident alacrity—into the mysteries of the craft. What I learned from them of the purely mechanical part of the process, together with what I have since added to it through the result of my own experiences, I shall now endeavour to communicate to my reader.

The piece it is intended to decorate must be in the clay state, that is to say, just as it leaves the hand of the potter, and before it has been submitted to any firing. Upon the still pulverulent and porous surface, the artist sketches freely the main lines of his subject. Then with a painting brush dipped in "Slip"—a term used in the trade for clay diluted with water to the consistency of a batter—he proceeds to lay on the foundations of his relief work. Coat after coat the slip is carefully applied; no fresh coat is to be added before the preceding one is perfectly dry. To neglect this precaution would be to compromise the success of the whole operation and cause the applied parts to blister or peel off from the ground.

With this preliminary brushwork a rough sketch is produced, in which care has to be taken to give to each part comparatively its right degree of relief; but the surface is rough and rugged, and no attempt has been made to introduce any detail. The work has now to be treated in the same way as a sculptor would treat a bas-relief of plaster of Paris or of fine grained stone. By means of sharp iron tools the substance is scraped, smoothed, incised, forms are softly modelled, details neatly defined, outlines made rigorously precise. As long as the artist is not satisfied, he may take the brush again and use it alternatively with the tool, raising one part, effacing another, as he may think it expedient. The last finishing touches, which shall preserve to the details a sharpness that glazing and firing would otherwise obliterate, are painted on with the thicker slip in a style quite peculiar to the treatment of *Pâte-sur-Pâte*. Although the clever management and happy graduations of the transparencies are only developed by vitrification, the operator has no other guide in that respect but his experience and judgement. Great disappointment may follow the firing of a piece, all miscalculations being first made manifest when it comes out of the oven. At that moment, unfortunately, it is too late to make any alteration; the work, once fired, can no longer be touched up; errors and misfortunes must stand as they are.

Solon at this stage discusses the various different bodies that can be used and after mentioning the French hard paste bodies, he continues:

A substitute has been found in England, where hard porcelain is not manufactured, in Parian, a body composed of the same elements combined in different proportions. Its greater fusibility allows of its being fired at a lower temperature than the one required by the Continental porcelain; and, under these conditions, many colours which cannot stand a higher degree of heat may be advantageously employed. . . .

As it is better that all pieces decorated by the process should be coloured through the mass, the body out of which they are to be fashioned has to be mixed with metallic oxides, incorporated by thorough grinding, in proportions varying from one to ten per cent. Occasionally, for instance, when a very strong tint is required—the proportion of oxide is increased, and a thin coat of the mixture is laid over the ground.

Solon then lists the various metallic oxides which were used to produce the ground colours on which the white reliefs were laid. He returns to the story of *pâte-sur-pâte* with an account of the firing process:

Pâte-sur-Pâte is baked in the same ovens and under the same conditions as the regular ware. The firing lasts about thirty-six hours, and after sufficient time has been allowed for cooling, the pieces are drawn out in the biscuit state. It has often been a matter of regret to me that some choice examples could not be left in that state. All the fineness of the workmanship can then be fully appreciated. In obedience to the established rule the biscuit has to be coated over with a transparent glaze of which lead forms the chief constituent.

When the pieces come out of the glost-oven (after glazing) they have passed through the last stage of manufacture; and although they may not be considered as satisfactory in all points, one must rest satisfied if they have not sustained such irretrievable accidents as renders them utterly worthless.

From the above account of this difficult and perilous process it will be readily understood that Solon's work was expensive. The single vase illustrated in Plate 91 took twenty-five days to make and the wholesale price in 1896 was a hundred and fifty guineas. In spite of these high prices the demand for *pâte-sur-pâte* was greater than the amount Solon could complete and in 1873 Mintons asked him to train apprentices.

The names of the following pupils are recorded: Alboine Birks, Lawrence Birks, H. Hollins, T. Mellor, A. Morgan, Frederick Rhead, T. H. Rice, H. Sanders and C. Toft.

At first these pupils were given simple floral subjects to complete and these were left unsigned. Later some of the pupils became highly proficient in their art while others found this particular style of decoration beyond them. As the fashion for *pâte-sur-pâte* was taken up by other manufacturers, Solon's pupils found themselves in great demand and were assured of constant employment.

It may be interesting to digress for a moment and to follow the fortunes of these nine apprentices. It is not only the incidence of alphabetical order that places the name of Alboine Birks at the head of the list, for he was to continue the tradition of Mintons' *pâte-sur-pâte* well into the twentieth century and gain for himself a reputation second only to Solon. Birks was born in the Potteries in 1861, and in 1876 at the age of fifteen he joined Mintons where he quickly proved to be Solon's ablest pupil. Solon himself was never prone to undue modesty and, as a result, the work of his pupils did not gain proper recognition until after his retirement. His general attitude towards his pupils is exemplified by his reply to one of them who sought permission to sign a specimen of his work. "Sign it! What for? My poor boy, people do *not* want to know if you have done it, all they want to know is that *I* have *not* done it."

Apart from his vases in the manner of Solon, Birks's name is associated with a charming system of decorating plates with panels of *pâte-sur-pâte*. To overcome the heavy appearance of a completely tinted plate he used a white plate into which recessed panels were worked and then filled with a tinted ground to receive the normal white *pâte-sur-pâte* decoration. This panelled work is of necessity on a small scale, but it is most attractive and found a ready market on both sides of the Atlantic. Richard Bradbury was trained by Birks to produce panelled plates and examples signed with the initials R.B. were worked by Bradbury in the twentieth century. Birks retired in 1937 and died on June 28th, 1941.

Lawrence A. Birks worked in a similar style to his cousin Alboine for a period of twenty-two years under Solon's guidance. Specimens of his work are signed L.B. but are much rarer than those of his cousin. Lawrence Birks set up a small factory—the Vine Pottery—close to Mintons in Stoke and took a partner by the name of Rawlins early in the twentieth century, the style then being Birks, Rawlins & Co.

H. Hollins, who signed his work with the initials H.H. produced some charming studies of children and cupids during the 1870's. Although his work is relatively scarce it is of fine quality and bears comparison with that of either Solon or Birks (Plate 83).

Little is known of Mellor, Morgan or Rice, apart from their names which appear in the Minton records.

Frederick Rhead, after being trained at Mintons, left their employment in 1877 at the age of twenty, and joined Wedgwood's staff. His work for this firm was shown at the 1878 Paris Exhibition. In 1887 he became Art Director for W. Brownfield & Sons. In 1888 Frederick Rhead decorated in *pâte-sur-pâte* an important Brownfield vase for presentation by the Staffordshire Liberals to W. E. Gladstone.

H. Sanders, after leaving Mintons, was employed at the Moore Brothers factory (St. Mary's Works) at Longton. This firm specialised in small pilgrim-shaped bottle vases decorated with *pâte-sur-pâte* figure subjects (Plate 84), and examples were shown at the Sydney International Exhibition of 1879. Sanders signed his work for Moore Brothers with his conjoined initials H.S.

Charles Toft, although listed as being trained by Solon in the *pâte-sur-pâte* technique, was mostly associated with the intricate inlaid copies of the early French Henri Deux ware. He later worked for Wedgwoods.

Returning to Solon—his work grew more and more popular and was exhibited at every international exhibition of the period. It would be tedious to quote from the many accounts of his successes published in the art journals of the period. There is, however, an interesting review of the Minton stand at the Paris Exhibition of 1878 contained in George Augustus Sala's *Paris Herself Again* which includes the following account and list of specimens: "The conspicuous exhibits in the interior are undeniably of the curious and delicate ceramic process known as *pâte-sur-pâte* executed by the gifted French artist M. Solon-Miles, who was formerly engaged at the State porcelain manufactory at Sèvres, but is now permanently domiciled on English soil. The very greatest care is necessary in manipulation and, the colours being opaque, the hand of a true artist is needed to fix the various gradations of light and shade. Among the principal examples of *pâte-sur-pâte* are an Etruscan vase, modelled from the original in the Museum at Naples, the subject, 'Cupid the Orator' on an olive green ground, understood to be the greatest work which M. Solon-Miles has yet produced; two vases with bas-reliefs of amorini on a celadon ground, the style of Louis Quatorze, some vases in the form of pilgrim bottles, the groups on which represent Cupid being instructed by a nymph, and Venus in the guise of a chiffonière picking up young lovers with her crocket; also a couple of arabesque vases decorated with graceful bas-reliefs, and exhibiting a clever combination of various coloured clays, and a bas-relief ornamental pink vase of a hue which the Sèvres manufactory has not yet sought to introduce. There are, moreover, a pair of vases of large dimensions, with cupids clustered round their stems, and encircled above by a ring of cupidons in *pâte-sur-pâte* engaged in demolishing chains of iron, and replacing them by chains of roses; also several delicate dessert plates, and a charming presse-papier, with a young maiden consigning her billets doux to the winds...."

The Art Student whose interesting rambles among the London china shops in 1876 have already been quoted in this book, contributes the following criticism of Solon's art: "Solon's work is now much sought after and is gradually rising in price, indeed so much so that I do not think I am alone in the belief that, great ceramic artist though he be, the prices his pieces now fetch are somewhat beyond their intrinsic value. I saw at Messrs. Daniells, Wigmore Street, and Messrs. Phillips and Pearce's and Messrs. Goode's some large vases ornamented by Solon, which were very handsome, the prices ranging about £200 the pair; but the two examples of his talent I thought most perfect were a pair of vases of moderate size, the ground being a beautiful shade of dark green, and a blue plaque with a cupid subject on it, entitled 'Thief.' The work of this artist varies considerably. In his larger subjects the figures are more perfect in outline and in higher relief than in his small ones, which are sometimes carelessly executed, thin and poor. His more recent efforts show a considerable advance on his earlier ones. . . . Of all ceramic artists now living in England, his reputation stands perhaps the highest. . . ."

Solon did not use models and each of his designs was original. A work book containing an outline sketch and title for each piece was kept at the factory, but in spite of many offers, Solon refused to make use of this to repeat any of his designs and, in consequence, every specimen of his work may be regarded as unique.

In 1904 Solon's long and successful association with Mintons came to an end. This did not mean the end of his career for, up to the time of his death in 1913, he continued to complete *pâte-sur-pâte* plaques in his own time. While employed in England Solon signed his work "L. Solon" or with a monogram. Apart from work in the *pâte-sur-pâte* technique he decorated a number of plaques with incised figure motifs, and an ornate overmantel at his home at Stoke was decorated by him with a series of incised plaques depicting allegorical figures of the Nations and their ceramic arts.

It was inevitable that other manufacturers, both in this country and on the continent, should try to repeat Mintons' success in the field of *pâte-sur-pâte* decoration, and reference has already been made to the productions of W. Brownfield & Sons and of the Moore Brothers. A passage in the *Pottery Gazette* of 1878 seems to imply that the Moore *pâte-sur-pâte* experiments date from about that time: "During a recent visit to the Potteries, we were pleased to see several good specimens of slip decoration or, as it is now called, *pâte-sur-pâte* at Messrs. Moore Brothers of Longton." These Moore examples however often display a badly crazed glaze, a general fault which occurs in other wares from this factory. Some examples of

81. BELLEEK ice-pail and cover in glazed and unglazed parian. Made for the Prince of Wales. *c.* 1868. Ht. 18 in.

82. MINTON plate, the centre pâte-sur-pâte panel by L. Birks. Date cypher for 1876.

88. MINTON pâte-sur-pâte plaque 'The Triumph of Cupid by M. L. Solon'. c. 1891. Length 16 in. Hove Museum of Art.

86. Three examples of MINTON pâte-sur-pâte decorated by M. L. SOLON's apprentices. *c.* 1875.

87. GEORGE JONES wall pockets decorated by F. Schenck. *c.* 1885. Ht. 8¾ in.

85. GRAINGER WORCESTER vase, pâte-sur-pâte decoration by E. Locke. *c*. 1880. (present owner unknown)

83. Pair of MINTON vases, the pâte-sur-pâte decoration by H. Hollins. *c.* 1878. Ht. 5½ in.

84. MOORE BROTHERS pilgrim bottles, the pâte-sur-pâte decoration by H. Sanders. *c.* 1880. Ht. 6½ in.

89. MINTON pâte-sur-pâte vase by Alboine Birks. Exhibited in 1894. Ht. 20 in.
Minton Works Museum.

Page 183

90
MINTON pâte-sur-pâte vase by A. Birks. *c.* 1890. (Present owner unknown.)

91
MINTON vase decorated by M. L. Solon in pâte-sur-pâte technique. *c.* 1895. Ht. 20 in. Mark No. 45. *In the possession of Messrs. Thomas Goode & Co.*

Page 184

92. Pair of MINTON pâte-sur-pâte vases by M. L. Solon, and a two piece vase with pâte-sur-pâte panels. c. 1898. *Victoria & Albert Museum.*

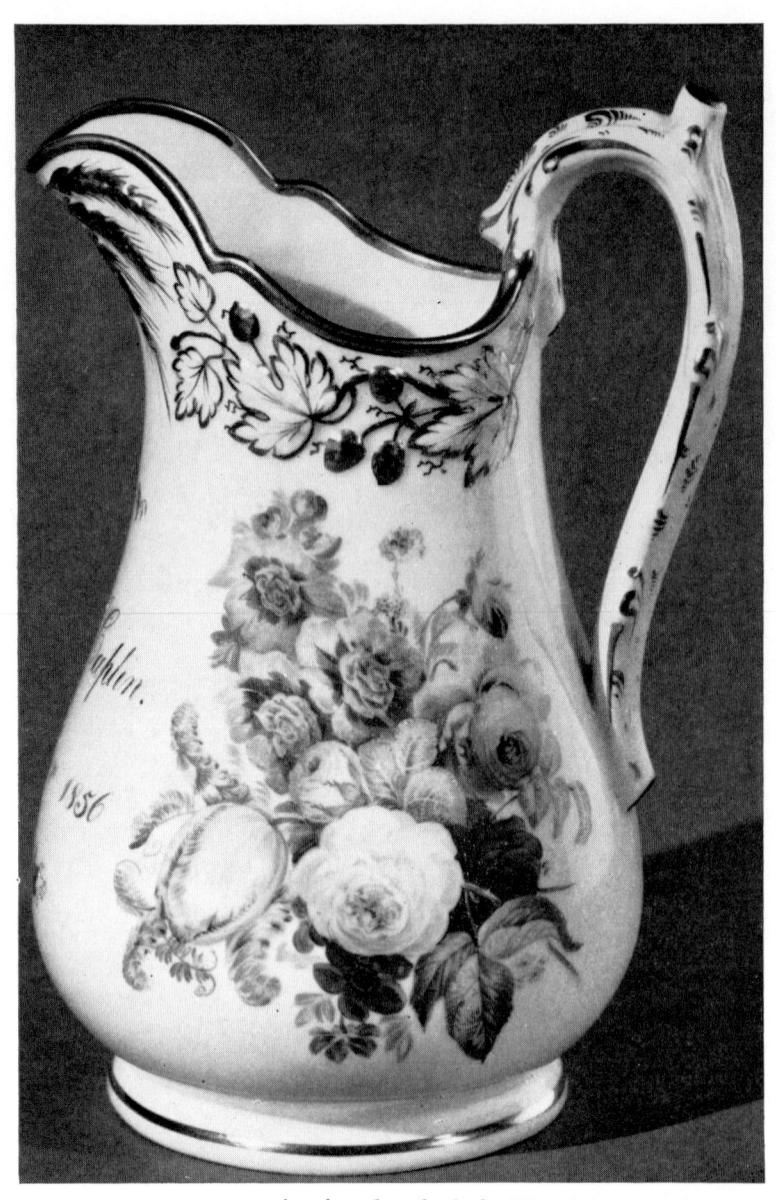

93. DAVENPORT presentation jug dated 1856. Ht. 7¾ in. Mark No. 73.

Moores' *pâte-sur-pâte* ware manufactured for the retailing firm of Thomas Goode and are inscribed in gold to this effect (Plate 84).

The Worcester factories were not slow to experiment with, and to produce, *pâte-sur-pâte* porcelains, but here the accent was on floral studies rather than figure motifs. The Worcester Royal Porcelain Company was fortunate in having on their staff a fine floral artist in Edward Raby, Senr. (both father and son were employed at the factory), who turned his attention to *pâte-sur-pâte* decoration in the 1870's. He generally used a lighter ground colour than those of Mintons, celadon ground being mentioned in accounts of the 1873 Vienna Exhibition.

The Grainger factory at Worcester also produced *pâte-sur-pâte* floral studies (Plate 85). Here the artist was Edward Locke whose initials can often be found incised into the bases of vases. Locke had a large family, some of whom were also employed in *pâte-sur-pâte* decoration for Graingers.

Many examples of rather heavily potted circular plaques and narrow vases are to be found decorated with *pâte-sur-pâte* motifs, generally of lightly clad females in or near water. These pieces were produced at George Jones's Trent Pottery (subsequently the Crescent Pottery), Stoke-on-Trent. An impressed mark consisting of the conjoined initials G.J. often over a large crescent, is usually indistinctly stamped on the bases of the vases or on the back of the plaques. Most examples lack the light touch so evident in the Minton pieces and this is probably due to the rather granular body and slip employed. The pieces have the appearance of earthenware as opposed to the porcelain or parian body employed elsewhere. Many of the compositions were used over and over again. The unusual pair of wall pockets illustrated in Plate 87 may be regarded as amongst the best specimens of George Jones' *pâte-sur-pâte*. These, like many other examples, bear the signature "Schenk Sc." Unlike other signatures which occur on *pâte-sur-pâte* wares Schenk's is never in white slip; it is incised into the coloured ground and consequently can be easily overlooked. Frederick Schenk was a well-known sculptor and modeller who worked also for Wedgwoods and for Brown-Westhead, Moore. He also taught modelling at the Hanley School of Art. In 1889 he was working in London where he designed many relief plaques for public buildings.

George Jones' *pâte-sur-pâte* mainly falls into the period 1876–86. The firm is mainly known for its "Majolica" glazed earthenware in the Minton tradition. George Jones himself was employed at Mintons until he established his own works at Stoke in 1861. He quickly built up a large trade and was especially concerned in exporting to North America.

With the notable exception of Mintons, the production of *pâte-sur-pâte* had ceased by 1890. This was due, not to a falling off in demand (as the overworked Birks would have been able to testify), but to the fact that this slow and painstaking method of decoration was not a practical proposition for the average manufacturer. As Solon himself has written, "they discovered to their cost that it did not bear mediocrity of execution".

CHAPTER 9

THE SMALLER FACTORIES

THIS chapter is devoted to some of the smaller manufacturers and to some miscellaneous subjects not dealt with elsewhere.

ROCKINGHAM

The Rockingham wares do not really belong to the Victorian era as the factory failed in 1842. Rare pieces of Rockingham marked "Manufacturers to the Queen", instead of the normal "Manufacturers to the King", were produced between 1837 and 1842. One of the workmen, Isaac Baguley, continued to decorate china on the site after the closure of the factory and used the normal Griffin mark with the addition of the words "Baguley, Rockingham Works"; his son Alfred succeeded his father and was still decorating in the mid-1860's. John Wager Brameld, an excellent artist and a former partner of the concern, also continued to decorate porcelain in the well-known Rockingham style up to the time of his death in 1851. Examples of his work were included in the 1851 Exhibition.

DAVENPORT

The Davenport factory at Longport, produced fine porcelain, earthenware and stone china from the end of the eighteenth century until the failure of the firm in 1887. Fine dessert services were a speciality of this factory and these were often decorated with landscapes. Richard Ablott and Jesse Mountford, both from the Derby factory, painted landscapes on Davenport porcelain. In the 1880's the factory specialised in colourful "Japan" patterns in the Derby style of the early part of the century, and a great quantity of tea sets were produced at this period. The Davenport earthenware and stone china was very durable, and for a long time the firm had the best reputation as suppliers of ships' crockery. Plaques may be found bearing the impressed mark "Davenport Patent", but it should not be assumed from this that these plaques were decorated at the factory or that the artist necessarily worked for Davenports, as a large number of undecorated plaques were sold to independent or amateur artists. These Davenport plaques proved most popular, since they were free from the distortion that was difficult to avoid in firing thin slabs of porcelain.

MOORE

The firm of Moore Brothers has been mentioned previously in connection with their *pâte-sur-pâte* pilgrim bottles. This firm dates back to 1830, when the title was Hamilton & Moore. In 1859 Samuel Moore became the sole proprietor of the St. Mary's Works, Longton, where a series of centrepieces, comports, candelabra and lamps were produced with applied plant motifs (especially of cacti). Moore Brothers (Bernard and Samuel from 1870) produced a good range of decorative porcelains and often used unusual bronze and metallic colours. Copies of Chinese cloisonné-enamel wares were also a feature of their work. Richard Pilsbury (from Mintons) was Art Director from 1892 until his death in 1897, and painted floral subjects in his well-known style (Plate 95). The works were sold in 1905; and subsequently Bernard Moore concentrated on wares with Chinese glaze effects which he produced at Wolfe Street, Stoke-on-Trent.

RIDGWAY

Many Victorian dessert services may be found bearing a large printed mark comprising the Royal Arms and the initials "J. R. & Co.". These wares were produced at the Cauldon Place factory in Hanley by John Ridgway, who was appointed Potter to the Queen. Pieces produced before 1830 bear the initials J.W.R. The entirely separate firm of Ridgway & Abington also produced porcelain wares.

BROWN-WESTHEAD, MOORE

The firm of Brown-Westhead, Moore, succeeded John Ridgway at Cauldon Place in 1855. Like their predecessors they were appointed Potters to the Queen and their products were shown in the international exhibitions of the period. Antonin Boullemier decorated fine porcelains for this firm after his break with Mintons. Other Cauldon Place artists include J.(?) Birbeck, T. J. Bott (about

1889), J. Ellis, C. Harrison, G. Landgraff, Legere, S. Pope and E. Sieffert. George Augustus Sala, writing of the firm's exhibits in the Paris Exhibition of 1878, noted, "Messrs. Brown-Westhead, Moore and Co. of Cauldon Place, exhibit decorative porcelain and pottery of a high order in great variety, including elegantly designed vases, well modelled representations of animals, colossal candelabra and brackets of much originality of form, many of these productions being distinguished, I may observe, by great boldness and breadth of design . . . several of the dessert services are decorated with designs from La Fontaine's fables, hunting subjects, and the like, and many of the vases are painted with figures and heads of animals."

When dating the later wares of this factory it is useful to remember that the firm was formed into a limited company in 1904, and the fact was recorded in the marks used after that date.

BROWNFIELD

W. Brownfield of Cobridge produced pottery from 1850. The manufacture of porcelain was somewhat belatedly introduced in 1871, but the excellence of the production compensated for the late start. Louis Jahn and Frederick Rhead (both of Mintons) were Art Directors here and themselves decorated some of the best work. In 1890 a Co-operative company was formed entitled Brownfield's Guild Pottery. The experiment failed after eight years and the works were demolished in 1898.

JAMES DUKE & NEPHEWS

Some excellent porcelain was produced during the 1860's by Sir James Duke & Nephews of the Hill Pottery, Burslem, who used a dexter hand as their trademark. The firm was founded about 1860 to take over the works of Samuel Alcock, who had been well known for such wares as moulded stoneware jugs. J. B. Waring in his review of the 1862 Exhibition, gives an account of their products: "Sir J. Duke and Nephews obtained at their first essay in the Arts, the distinction of a prize medal. . . . From among the great variety of works produced by them we have selected a portion of the dessert service executed in porcelain and parian, very beautifully designed by Mr. G. Eyre, the figures excellently modelled by Mr. Giovanni Meli, and very prettily set-off with coloured flowers and ornaments, delicately painted. They have been fortunate in obtaining the services of Mr. E. [sic] Protat, the well-known French sculptor and modeller. Mr. W. Slater who paints most of their enamel subjects in the Limoges style, is also deserving of great praise. . . . We must not omit to praise also the parian statuettes, the Cupid Captive, modelled by Mr. Calder Marshall, the eminent sculptor, and Marmion, by Mr. Bailly. The parian foliage and fruit ornament on vases and ewers by Mr. W. Parker evinced very delicate manipulation and a lively fancy." The review also mentions the firm's "Majolica" and "Etruscan" pieces. After such a description it is surprising to learn that this firm lasted for only five years.

BELLEEK

The wares from the Belleek factory (County Fermanagh, Northern Ireland) have gained popularity in recent years. Typical specimens have an iridescent glaze well suited to their marine forms and patterns. The date of the establishment of this factory is variously given as 1857 and 1863, but trials of local Irish clays had been carried out in the early 1850's at the Worcester factory at the request of R. W. Armstrong and the promising results suggested to him that a factory could be established near the source of the material. As a result Armstrong took a partner, David McBirney (under whose name the factory traded), and established a factory at Belleek. The Belleek wares were first introduced to the public at the Dublin International Exhibition of 1865. Typical marine patterns were registered with the Patent Office from 1868 onwards. R. W. Armstrong (b. 1824, d. 1884) acted as Art Director and was responsible for the marine motifs. Ornate services were made for Queen Victoria and the Prince of Wales in the 1870's. The centre-pieces, comports and ice pails (Plate 81) were designed to contrast with good effect the matt unglazed parian-like body with the rich irridescence of the glazed portions. Some charming figures and groups were also produced showing this contrast of effects. In 1878 some two hundred hands were employed at the factory although in 1865 the number had been only about seventy, of which thirty were boys or girls. Dessert, tea and cabaret sets were produced, and some of the teaware was remarkably thinly potted. The skilful workmanship was perhaps best displayed in a series of openwork baskets with floral encrustation such pieces are still produced to-day.

GOSS

The name of Goss has lost prestige in the last fifty years owing to the flood of cheap crested holiday mementos produced by this firm. In Victorian times, however, William Henry Goss of Stoke-on-Trent was responsible for some fine "art productions", including floral jewellery, busts and figures. Jewelled and hand painted vases in the Goss ivory body were also noteworthy. The works were established in 1858 and its wares have a great similarity in body and glaze to the Irish Belleek porcelain.

DOULTON (BURSLEM)

In 1877 the Lambeth firm of Doulton, which had been known for many years for its stoneware and earthenware, took over a separate factory at Burslem for the production of fine earthenware and porcelain. The firm's porcelain soon became popular, especially in the North American markets and it proved particularly successful at the Chicago Exhibition of 1893. Some of the leading artists employed at Burslem were Percy Curnock (worked 1885-1919); David Dewsbury (worked 1889-1919); Fred Hancock (worked 1879-1913); Charles Hart (worked 1880-1927); Henry Mitchell (worked 1893-1908); Edward Raby, of Worcester (worked 1892-1919); Walter Slater (worked 1880-1910); George White (worked 1885-1912) and Sam Wilson (worked 1880-1909). These, and other artists employed, usually signed their work in full.

WEDGWOOD

The Wedgwood firm which was mainly known for its earthenwares and stonewares, re-introduced in 1878 a bone-china porcelain body, similar to one it had made for a short period early in the century. Mintons' figure painter, Thomas Allen, was engaged at this period, and decorated both earthenware and the re-introduced porcelain wares until his retirement, about 1900. Acid gilding in the Minton tradition was also practised at Wedgwoods.

In contrast to the finely painted decoration on Minton and other factory porcelain the collector of Victorian ceramics will often come across examples with a decidedly amateur appearance, lacking in design and drawing, and painted with dull muddy colours. These are indeed amateur decorated pieces, for during the 1870's and 1880's a craze swept the country for the home painting of porcelain; and the vogue was further encouraged by the publicity given to Mintons' Art-Pottery Studio in Kensington Gore (Chapter 5). The London retailers, Howell & James, held annual exhibitions of work by amateurs from 1876. These exhibitions were extremely popular and were patronised by Queen Victoria and other members of the Royal Family. A contemporary advertisement reads "The exhibition of 1878 contained upwards of 1,000 original works—mostly by ladies—and was frequented during its two months' duration by nearly 10,000 visitors. . . ." Examples of amateur work can occasionally be found still bearing the original paper label of Howell & James giving details of the painter, source of design and date. Similar exhibitions were held up and down the country and several books were published giving instruction on ceramic painting. Various manufacturers catered for this trade by supplying undecorated blanks; in particular examples with Mintons' impressed mark and date cyphers are often found. The amateur artists invariably signed and dated their efforts, which have a special interest in that the paintings were not influenced by factory traditions or by commercial requirements. Gilt edges associated with factory products are noticeably absent on amateur decorated pieces.

Mention was made in Chapter 7 of the various Art Unions which helped so much to publicise the parian body. The activities of Henry Cole's "Summerly's Art Manufactures", founded in 1847, had a similar effect. In 1846 Henry Cole, using the pseudonym "Felix Summerly" won a Society of Arts prize for a simply designed teaset, which was made in earthenware by Mintons. Encouraged by this success Cole engaged leading designers and artists to design everyday utilitarian wares. The *Art Union* magazine contained the following comments in the June 1847 issue: "We direct attention to an advertisement which announced that 'Felix Summerly' has induced several of the most eminent British artists to make designs for British manufacturers—a course we have strongly advocated for years, and earnestly hoped to see accomplished. We shall, therefore, cordially rejoice if the gentleman to whom we refer, and who in experience, taste and judgement is second to none, can succeed in so wedding 'High Art' to the Art that has been in this country considered and treated as 'Low Art', so as to commence a new era for both." Later in 1847 the same journal follows up the original announcement: "We rejoice that Felix Summerly has succeeded in inducing such men as Mulready, Maclise, Redgrave, Horsley, Townsend, Bell and others, to aid in a project pregnant with immensly beneficial results to British Manufactured Art. . . . We understand that arrangements are making to carry out this project upon a very extensive scale, and that ere long, there will be few of the manufacturers of England who will not contribute to it, in one form or another. . . . We are glad to hear that her Majesty has manifested an interest in Summerly's Art Manufactures . . . we understand her Majesty was pleased to become the purchaser of all the more important works of the series."

Like many promising ideas, the scheme did not receive the support that might have been expected. The *Art Union* magazine rapidly changed its opinion and published many scathing remarks, both with regard to the design of the specimens and to Henry Cole's dictatorial conditions imposed on the manufacturers responsible for producing his wares. In addition the "Summerly" products did not enjoy a ready sale. "In hardly one instance have they remunerated the manufacturer, in fact, the only selling object of the entire collection is the statuette of Mr. Bell's 'Dorothea'" (*Art Union*, 1848). 'Dorothea' is illustrated in Plate 71. The "Summerly's Art Manufactures" lasted for only three years. Henry Cole then became engaged in the preparations for the forthcoming 1851 Exhibition, and served on the executive committee. The "Summerly" wares, ranging from ceramics to papier-mâché and silver objects, are usually marked. The mark used on the parian figures made for him by Mintons is reproduced on page 116.

Among the Victorian wares with a specialised interest, mention must be made of the small unpretentious porcelain plaques moulded with a recessed pattern. On holding these pieces up to a strong light, the picture comes to life in striking effects of light and shade. These porcelain plaques, called lithophanes or transparencies, were very popular in the middle of the nineteenth century and were mounted in windows, clipped in front of candles and mounted in sets to form a lamp shade. The great majority of them were made on the Continent, but various English manufacturers produced them under licence. At Mintons they were referred to as "Berlin Transparencies". The subjects were usually portraits, landscapes, figure subjects or copies of Old Masters. A list discovered at Mintons, dated February 1850, gives the following titles of Minton examples: "The Penitent", "Naomi and her daughters-in-law", "Mother and

Child", "Guardian Angel", "Quentin Durward", "Mother and Dying Child", "The Agony in the Garden", "The Jolly Good Fellow" and "The Offering". In addition to Mintons, they were also produced by a firm called Adderley & Lawson, by Copelands, by Grainger (of Worcester) and by a small factory at Llanelly in South Wales. Although most lithophanes were produced in the 1850's a certain Robert Griffiths Jones took out a British Patent for a process of making them as early as 1828.

It may be noticed that little reference has been made to porcelain figures, apart from the Worcester examples (Chapter 6) and the many parian models. The "student" remarked in 1876: "In the ordinary china shop, figures form a prominent feature amongst the ornamental portion of the stock, but in high class pottery" (a term used loosely by the writer for both pottery and porcelain) "figures are the exception. Vases, plaques, plates, cups and saucers and bottles I saw in plenty but the only high class figures I observed were either Worcester or Dresden. . . ."

A considerable number of painted porcelain plaques were produced during this period. Besides their decorative interest such plaques may be of great value from the student's point of view; for the artist was more inclined to sign and date a plaque, which he treated as a work of fine art, than to sign a vase or plate. Plaques can therefore be of considerable documentary importance and in some cases may represent the only signed examples of an artist's work. This is so in the case of two of the plaques illustrated, Plates 99 & 102.

It is important to notice that some of the finest wares were often made especially for the United States of America where Victorian porcelain was appreciated and found a remunerative market. J. M. O'Fallon writing in the *Art Journal* of 1897 refers to this aspect of porcelain design: "It is well known that for years past choice examples of fictile ware, as well as high class other kinds of articles of British handicraft, have found ready sale in America; but we are scarcely prepared to learn, during a recent visit to the potteries, that the chief firms were paying altogether special attention to American orders; some of the old established London dealers in china and glass, such as Phillips, Goode, Mortlock, Daniell, who mainly supply the nobility and gentry, have their own pick of artistic pottery from Staffordshire and from Worcester, Derby, Coalport, and elsewhere, but the fact remains that America is at the present hour the purchaser of the most costly work and, to a very large extent, of the better class general pottery of English make. Noted manufacturers like Minton, Copeland, Wedgwood, Brown-Westhead, Moore & Co., Doulton & Co. (Burslem), Brownfield, Moore Bros., apart from their specially decorative pieces, are now busy catering for American requirements which differ somewhat from English in a few particulars. . . . Fish and game are painted after nature: fishes and marine views, and plants for the fish plates; birds, flowers, insects and landscapes for the game plates; fruits, flowers and, now and again, cupids and other figures for the dessert plates. In prevailing colour-tone as in design, each of a dozen differs from the rest in all but edge, which is generally of raised irregular scroll-work, gilt. Many of the table services are in blue and gold, or grey and gold, but the leading colour of these for the American market is green of several shades, nearly always heightened with gold. In the latter kinds Copeland's and Doulton's and George Jones are also very strong. As we have said above, the more artistic and costly products of Staffordshire fictile ware also find ready sale in America. They chiefly consist of vases, some of which are valued at hundreds of pounds. A pair of these were sold for £1,600; they were in *pâte-sur-pâte*, and from the hands of Solon, the principal artist at Minton's works. . . ."

These fine porcelain wares, which were made in Britain for the United States of America, are an instance of the close connection which has existed in the nineteenth century, and later, between the decorative arts of the two countries.

BROWN-WESTHEAD, MOORE ARTISTS

BERNARD. Floral, bird and fish painter. Late nineteenth century.
BIRBECK, J.(?). Fish and game subjects. Late nineteenth century.
BOTT, THOMAS JOHN. Enamel painting, c. 1885-9. See Coalport and Worcester.
BOULLEMIER, ANTONIN. Born c. 1840, d. 1900. See also Mintons.
DAVIES, E. Late nineteenth century.
DUTTON, J. Late nineteenth century.
EDWARDS, THOMAS. Floral artist. Late nineteenth century.
ELLIS, JOSEPH. Landscape artist. Late nineteenth century.
HARRISON, C. Late nineteenth century.
HILLMAN. Late nineteenth century.
JOHNSON, W. Late nineteenth century.

LANDGRAFF, G. Figure painter, *c.* 1865–80 (later at Derby).
LEGER(E). Late nineteenth century.
LEONCE, G. Fruit, floral and bird subjects, *c.* 1875–80.
MALLET, P. Fruit and floral artist, *c.* 1875–90.
NIXON, GEORGE. Late nineteenth century.
PALMER, E. Late nineteenth century.
POPE, S. Late nineteenth century.
SCHENCK, F. Modeller. Late nineteenth century.
SIEFFERT, E. Sèvres trained figure painter, from 1887.
STEELE, H. Late nineteenth century.
TAYLOR, W. Late nineteenth century.

DAVENPORT ARTISTS

ABLOTT, RICHARD. Formerly at Derby, *c.* 1870–80.
EATON, R. Floral artist, *c.* 1880.
FLETCHER, W. Figure painter, *c.* 1830–50.
MARSH, JAMES. Modeller, mid-nineteenth century.
MOUNTFORD, JESSE. Scenic artist from Derby and Coalport, *c.* 1840–61, d. 1861.
SLATER, WILLIAM. Apprenticed at Derby, *c.* 1850–60, d. 1864.
SLATER, WILLIAM, JUNIOR. Born 1807. Decorator, *c.* 1833–65, d. 1865.
STEELE, THOMAS. Born 1772. Floral and fruit painter from Derby, *c.* 1820. Later for Mintons, d. 1850.

DOULTON (BURSLEM) ARTISTS
(Victorian Period only)

ALLEN, HARRY. From *c.* 1899 into twentieth century, d. 1951.
ALLEN, ROBERT. Gilder and designer from *c.* 1877 into twentieth century, d. 1934.
ASH, A. Late nineteenth century.
BETTELEY, HARRY. Late nineteenth, early twentieth century.
BILTON, R. Late nineteenth, early twentieth century.
BIRBECK, HARRY. Fish and game subjects from 1900. Retired *c.* 1922.
BIRKS, EDWARD. Floral artist, *c.* 1875–89.
BROWN, WILMOT. Landscape painter, *c.* 1879 into twentieth century.

CURNOCK, PERCY. Born 1872. Floral and landscape artist from 1885 into twentieth century, d. 1956.
DEWSBERRY, DAVID. Born 1851. Floral artist (orchids) from 1889 into twentieth century, d. 1956.
EATON, ARTHUR. Born 1875. Landscape and figure artist from 1889 into twentieth century, d. 1933.
HANCOCK, FRED. Fish and game subjects from 1879–1913.
HOPKINS, C. B. Landscapes, etc., from 1895 into twentieth century.
MITCHELL, HENRY. Landscapes and animal subjects from 1893–1908.
NOKE, C. J. Modeller, mainly twentieth century, d. 1954.
PIPER, HARRY. Rose painter. Late nineteenth, early twentieth century.
PLANT, JOHN H. Scenic artist, from Coalport.
RABY, EDWARD. Floral artist from 1892–1919. From Worcester.
SLATER, JOHN. Art Director, decorator from *c.* 1877 into twentieth century.
SLATER, WALTER. Floral subjects from 1880–1910.
WHITE, GEORGE. Figure painter from 1885–1912.
WILSON, SAM. Landscape and cattle subjects from 1880–1909.

GENERAL MARKS

	Mark No.	
B.W.M.	69	Brown-Westhead, Moore. Various printed or impressed marks incorporating the initials B.W.M. or "Cauldon". *c.* 1862+.
W.B. W B & S.	70 & 71	Brownfields, *c.* 1871+. Various printed or impressed marks, incorporating the initials W.B. or the title "Brownfield Guild Pottery". Impressed date cyphers occur.

Coalport. See Chapter 2.

Copeland } See
Copeland & Garrett } Chapter 3

Mark
No.

72 Davenport. Early Victorian printed mark.

73 Davenport. Printed mark mainly used *c.* 1850–70, but occasionally occurs on pre-1830 pieces.

DAVENPORT
LONGPORT
STAFFORDSHRE

74 Davenport. Late printed mark, *c.* 1870–80.

DAVENPORT PATENT 74a Davenport. Impressed mark on plaques, see page 189.

— Derby. See Chapter 4.

DOULTON 75 Doulton impressed on Burslem porcelain from *c.* 1877.

76 Doulton. Printed mark from *c.* 1877. "England" added *c.* 1891. Mark occurs with, or without, crown above.

77 Doulton. Late printed mark (*c.* 1902 onwards).

12 . 2 . 01. 78 Doulton. Impressed date cyphers. Day. Month. Last two figures of year, e.g. 12 February 1901.

Mark No.

DOULTON PATTERN NUMBERS

contd. On the introduction of porcelain at the Burslem factory a system of pattern numbers bearing the prefix "C" (for China) was introduced. By January 1st, 1900 the number reached was C.9138. In October 1901 a new series, bearing the prefix "E" came into use and in December 1915 the present "H" series commenced.

In many cases specimens of Doulton porcelain will be found bearing two different sets of numbers. One will be the factory reference number bearing the single letter prefix as explained above. The other is the department reference number prefixed by the initials of the foreman artist, i.e. R.A. (Robert Allen), H.B. (Herbert Betteley), H.N. (Harry Nixon)—each department having its own set of patterns.

— Grainger (Worcester). See Chapter 6.

— Hadley (Worcester). See Chapter 6.

— Hancock (Derby). See Chapter 4.

79 George Jones printed or impressed mark, 1861+. Found on all types of wares, sometimes initials only. "England" may be added after 1891.

— Kerr & Binns (Worcester). See Chapter 6.

— Locke (Worcester). See Chapter 6.

— Minton. See Chapter 5.

	Mark No.	
MOORE	80	Moore Brothers. Impressed mark *c.* 1870+. "England" occurs from 1891.
	81	Moore Brothers. Printed mark *c.* 1880+. "England" added *c.* 1891.
	—	Registration mark. See Appendix I.
WEDGWOOD	82	Wedgwood. Printed mark on porcelain from 1878. "England" added *c.* 1891. Stars occur under the Portland vase mark and would seem to indicate a late date. "Bone China" added under Wedgwood, *c.* 1900.
WEDGWOOD	83	Impressed mark also found on porcelain, from 1878.

PATTERN NUMBERS ON WEDGWOOD PORCELAIN

Prefix X Dinnerware 1879–1919.
„   Y Teaware 1879–1931.
„   Z Ornamental pieces 1879 onwards.

94. Clock case made by Moore Brothers. *c.* 1890. Length 10 in. Mark No. 81.

95
Centrepiece made by
Moore Brothers
painted with orchids
by Richard Pilsbury.
c. 1895. Length 14½ in.
Mark No. 81.

96
DOULTON (Burslem)
vase painted by
George White.
c. 1900. Ht. 11 in.
Mark No. 77

97. Plate made by John Ridgway & Bates. *c.* 1856–8. *Victoria & Albert Museum.*

98. DOULTON (Burslem) service plate with raised gilding designed by Robert Allen. *c.* 1890. (Copyright Royal Doulton Potteries.)

99
Porcelain plaque signed 'J. Mountford 1851', the Derby and Davenport scenic painter.

100
Porcelain plaque signed 'Wm. Corden', the Derby trained scenic and figure painter.

Page 207

101
Porcelain plaque signed 'T. Simpson', the Minton floral painter.

102
Porcelain plaque signed 'John Randall, F.G.S. Coalport Nov. 1870'.

Page 208

CHAPTER 10

NOTES ON DATING

THE various marks used by the principal manufacturers of the period are given at the end of the relevant chapters. These marks, especially when they are found in conjunction with a factory date cypher, give a ready guide to dating.

REGISTRATION MARKS

A diamond shaped mark, either printed or impressed into the ware is often found on Victorian ceramics of the period 1842/1883. This mark indicates that the shape or pattern was registered with the Patent Office in London to prevent copying by other manufacturers. From this mark, the date on which the pattern was first registered can be ascertained (see Appendix I). It should always be borne in mind that the date given in the table is not necessarily the date when the piece was made, for a popular pattern would continue to be produced for some time after the date of its first introduction and registration. This is particularly the case when it was the shape, or form of pierced border, that was the subject of registration. Occasionally continental manufacturers registered their patterns in England and the mark cannot therefore be accepted as proof of English manufacture.

The diamond shaped device was abolished in 1883. From January 1884 a simple system of consecutive numbering was introduced commencing with I. By January 1900 the registration number had reached 351202. Any ceramic object bearing a numerical registration number—usually prefixed "Rd. No."—cannot date from before 1884. It should be noted that these numbers were not confined to ceramics but applied to all classes of ware, e.g. metal objects, glass and textiles, whereas in the earlier system the productions were divided into classes and the class number (earthenware and porcelain was class IV) appeared at the top of the diamond mark.

PATTERN NUMBERS

Pattern numbers occur on many pieces of Victorian ceramics. Their purpose was to facilitate re-ordering or matching and for this reason these numbers are not a reliable indication of date. Many of the specimens decorated by the leading artists of the period do not bear any pattern number as they were individual pieces not intended to be repeated.

The early patterns were numbered consecutively until a figure such as 9999 was reached when a second series was employed. These were of two kinds: the more usual method was to use a letter prefix i.e. G.1 to G.9999 (as employed by Mintons in the second half of the nineteenth century); the second method was to express the pattern number in fractional form i.e. $\frac{3}{456}$, where the 3 indicates that the pattern number 456 is from the third series or from the third pattern book. These two distinctive forms can be of assistance in attributing, often in a negative way, unmarked pieces, for a plate bearing a "fractional" pattern number could not have been produced by Copelands, Mintons or any of the firms which employed the prefix system.

Sample forms of pattern numbers with relevant dates are incorporated under each factory's table of marks but these should only be regarded as an approximate guide. All pattern numbers are painted or printed over the glaze. Impressed or incised numbers refer to the shape, mould number or size of the article.

"ENGLAND"

To comply with the American McKinley Tariff Act of 1891 the word "ENGLAND" was added to most factory marks in that year. This gives a valuable guide to dating the products of the smaller factories during the 1880's and 1890's. "MADE IN ENGLAND" generally denotes a date after 1900.

DEALERS' MARKS

Mid-Victorian wares often bear printed marks incorporating the names of the firms of Daniell, Goode or Mortlock who were the leading London retailers of the period and who often commissioned special pieces or purchased the whole output of some particular pattern. Daniells were the main agents for Coalport porcelain. Goodes specialised in products of the Minton factory. Marks of various smaller retailers are also found, especially those of a group trading in the vicinity of St. Paul's Churchyard.

A misconception often arises over the figures "51" found in the centre of the normal Royal Worcester mark. These figures refer to the establishment of the factory in 1751 and have no connection whatsoever with the 1851 Exhibition. In fact, this mark was not used until the Kerr & Binns period which commenced in 1852 (see pages 124 and Mark No. 51, page 141).

The date A.D. 1750 incorporated in some of the late Coalport productions has of course no relevance to the date of manufacture but refers to the date claimed for the establishment of the firm.

Many impressed marks and date cyphers are indistinct but can often be deciphered if held to a strong light with the marks outermost.

The period of the main porcelain manufacturers can be readily found from the table in Appendix II.

APPENDIX I

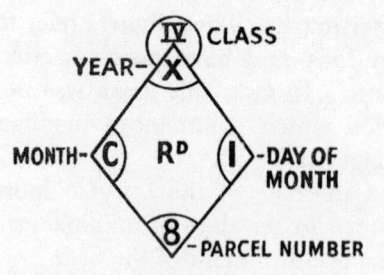

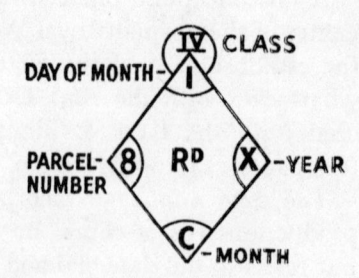

Pattern Registered Jan. 1st, 1842   Pattern Registered Jan. 1st, 1868

Above are the two patterns of Design Registration Marks that were in current use between the years 1842 and 1883. Keys to "year" and "month" code-letters are given below. These Marks were used only when a particular design was registered at the Patent Office. The left-hand diamond was used during the years 1842 to 1867. A change was made in 1868 when the right-hand diamond was adopted. (See page 209)

INDEX TO YEAR AND MONTH LETTERS

YEARS

1842–67		1868–83	
Year Letter at Top		*Year Letter at Right*	
A = 1845	N = 1864	A = 1871	L = 1882
B = 1858	O = 1862	C = 1870	P = 1877
C = 1844	P = 1851	D = 1878	S = 1875
D = 1852	Q = 1866	E = 1881	U = 1874
E = 1855	R = 1861	F = 1873	V = 1878
F = 1847	S = 1849	H = 1869	W = (Mar.
G = 1863	T = 1867	I = 1872	1-6) 1878
H = 1843	U = 1848	J = 1880	X = 1868
I = 1846	V = 1850	K = 1883	Y = 1879
J = 1854	W = 1865		
K = 1857	X = 1842		
L = 1856	Y = 1853		
M = 1859	Z = 1860		

APPENDIX I

MONTHS (BOTH PERIODS)

A = December
B = October
C or O = January
D = September
E = May

G = February
H = April
I = July
K = November (& December 1860)

M = June
R = August (& September 1st–19th 1857)
W = March

It will be noted that there are several departures from the general pattern in the above keys. In the year-dates, letter W in the right-hand column was used only for the brief period March 1st to 6th. For the rest of that year, 1878, the letter D applied. Similarly in the "Months" column—for the year 1860 only—the November code letter K was used to include the first eight days of December, with the letter A applying to the rest of December. The same thing occurs again with R, the letter representing August. In 1857 only, the letter R continued to be used into September until the 19th, the letter D being used for the remaining days of the month.

The above exceptions are as accurate as can be ascertained from careful investigation and research of contemporary records and sources of information. The reasons for them are not known.

In 1884 a more simple system of consecutive numbering was introduced:

TABLE OF DESIGN REGISTRATION NUMBERS FROM 1884 TO 1901

The following numbers are the first issued in January of each year; but it should be noted that previous to the beginning of 1892 a slight numerical overlap occurs between the registrations of each December and January.

	Rd. No.		Rd. No.		Rd. No.
1884	1	1890	141273	1896	268392
1885	19754	1891	163767	1897	291241
1886	40480	1892	185713	1898	311658
1887	64520	1893	205240	1899	331707
1888	90483	1894	224720	1900	351202
1889	116648	1895	246975	1901	368154

APPENDIX II

TABLE OF THE MAIN
VICTORIAN PORCELAIN MANUFACTURERS

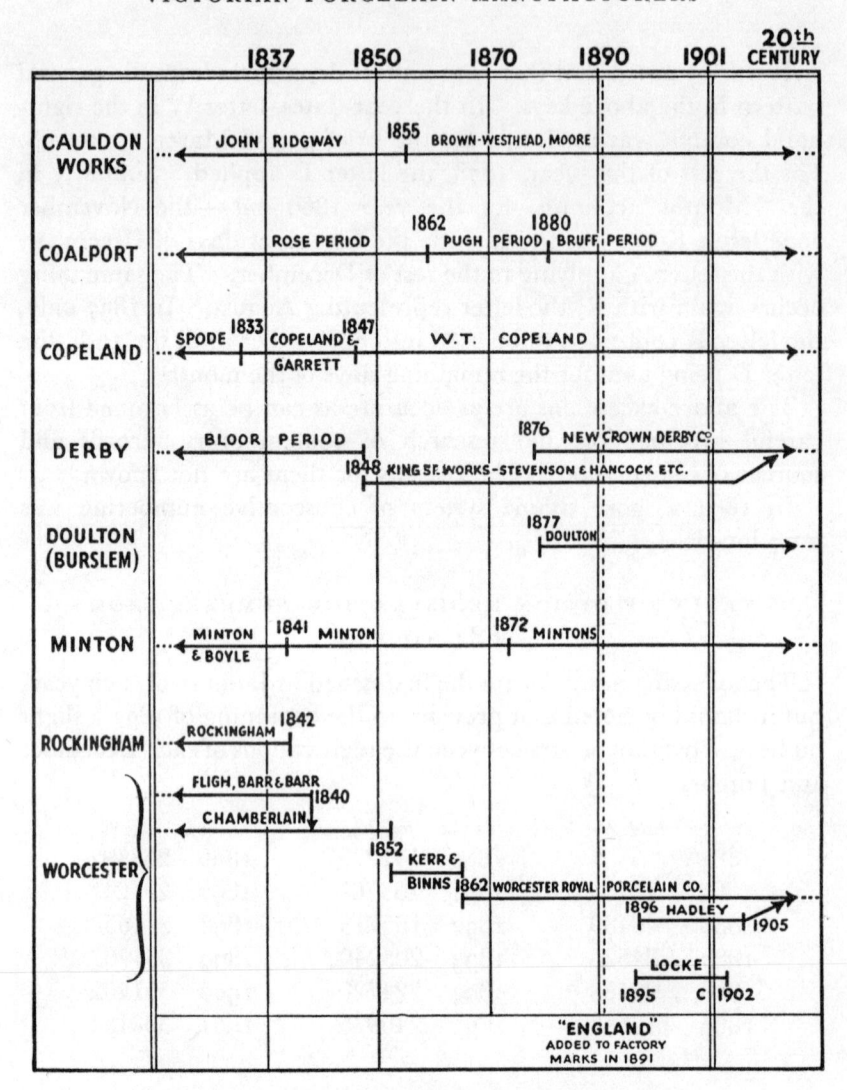

	1837	1850	1870	1890	1901	20th CENTURY
CAULDON WORKS	←— JOHN RIDGWAY	**1855** BROWN-WESTHEAD, MOORE				—→
COALPORT	←— ROSE PERIOD	**1862** PUGH PERIOD	**1880** BRUFF PERIOD			—→
COPELAND	←— SPODE **1833** COPELAND & GARRETT **1847**	W.T. COPELAND				—→
DERBY	←— BLOOR PERIOD		**1876** NEW CROWN DERBY CO.			—→
		1848 KING ST. WORKS - STEVENSON & HANCOCK ETC.				
DOULTON (BURSLEM)			**1877** DOULTON			—→
MINTON	←— MINTON & BOYLE **1841** MINTON	**1872** MINTONS				—→
ROCKINGHAM	←— ROCKINGHAM **1842**					
WORCESTER	←— FLIGH, BARR & BARR **1840** CHAMBERLAIN	**1852** KERR & BINNS **1862** WORCESTER ROYAL PORCELAIN CO.		**1896** HADLEY **1905**		—→
				LOCKE **1895** C **1902**		
				"ENGLAND" ADDED TO FACTORY MARKS IN 1891		

Note the S added to the MINTON mark in 1872

214

SELECTED BIBLIOGRAPHY

Art Union, from 1839 to 1848, afterwards entitled the *Art Journal*.
Art Journal, from 1849.
Masterpieces of Industrial Art & Sculpture (3 vols.). J. B. Waring. 1862.
The Old Derby China Factory. J. Haslem. 1876.
Pottery Gazette—a Trade Journal from 1877.
Pottery and Porcelain in 1876. Anonymous (Published by Field & Tuer). 1877.
Worcester Pottery and Porcelain 1751–1851. R. W. Binns. 1877.
Ceramic Art of Great Britain. L. Jewitt. 1878. (Revised edition 1883.)
Magazine of Art, from 1878 to 1902.
Paris Herself Again (2 vols.). G. A. Sala. 1879.
Worcester China 1852–1897. R. W. Binns. 1897.
History and Description of English Porcelain. W. Burton. 1902.
Staffordshire Pots and Potters. G. W. & F. A. Rhead. 1906.
Nineteenth Century English Ceramic Art. J. F. Blacker. 1911.
Pottery and Glass—a Trade Journal from 1918.
Spode and his Successors. A. Hayden. 1925.
Marks and Monograms on European and Oriental Pottery and Porcelain. William Chaffers. 14th Edit., 1954.
Caughley and Coalport Porcelain. F. A. Barrett. 1951.
Crown Derby Porcelain. F. B. Gilhespy. 1951.
The House of Coalport 1750–1950. Compton Mackenzie. 1951.
Victorian and Edwardian Decorative Arts. V. & A. Exhibition Catalogue. 1952.
Nineteenth Century English Pottery and Porcelain. G. Bemrose. 1953.
Handbook of Pottery and Porcelain Marks. J. B. Cushion & W. B. Honey. 1956.
Connoisseur Period Guide—Early Victorian (Chapter on "Pottery, Porcelain and Glass" by H. Wakefield). 1958.
Victorian Pottery and Porcelain. G. B. Hughes. 1959.
Connoisseur Concise Encyclopaedia of Antiques, Vol. IV (article on "English Ceramic Artists of the Victorian Era" by G. Godden). 1959.

Interesting specimens of Victorian ceramics may be seen at the Stoke-on-Trent Museum & Art Gallery, Hanley, and at the Victoria

& Albert Museum, London. The Museums attached to the Copeland, Minton and Royal Worcester Works contain a fine selection of their respective products. Messrs. Wengers Ltd. of Etruria (Manufacturers of ceramic colours, etc.) have an interesting collection. Some documentary exhibition specimens of Victorian ceramics can be seen in the showrooms of Messrs. Thomas Goode & Co. in South Audley Street, London, W.1.

INDEX

A

Ablott, R., 42, 75, 189, 198
Abraham, R. F., *Pls. 7, 9*; 25, 27, 40-1, 43, 50, 53
Abraham, R. J., 51, 53
Acid Gilding, 94, 194
Adams, F. W., 53
Adams, W. & Sons, *Pl. 78*
Adderley & Lawson, 196
Alcock, S., *Pls. 21, 23*; 51-2, 53
Alcock, Messrs. S., 24, 191
Allen, H., 198
Allen, R., *Pl. 98*; 198, 201
Allen, T., *Pls. 34, 35, 41*; 25, 27, 92, 103, 193
Amateur decoration, 193-4
American market, 196-7
Armstrong, R. W., 192
Arnoux, L., *Pl. 42*; 91-2, 103, 162
Arrowsmith, J., 51, 53
Art Pottery Studio, 97-8, 194
Art Unions, *Pl. 69*; 147-50
Ash, A., 198
Aston, J., 41, 43

B

Baguley, A., 189
Baguley, I., 189
Bailly, (?), 192
Baker, (?), 123, 139
Baldwyn, C. H. C., 139
Ball, E. O., 42, 43
Ball, T., 53
Bancroft, J., 53, 68, 89, 103
Barnet, J., 75
Barr Porcelain, 142
Bates, D., 123, 139
Battam, F., 53
Battam, T., 48, 50, 53, 147, 148, 151, 152
Bayley, E. S., 103
Beard, J., 42, 43
Bejot, E., 139
Bell, J., *Pls. 70, 71, 73*; 103, 116, 164
Belleek, *Pl. 81*; 27, 163, 192
Berlin Transparencies, 195-6

Bernard, (?), 197
Besche, L., *Pl. 19*; 27, 51, 53, 99, 103
Betteley, H., 198, 201
Bilton, R., 198
Binns, A., 139
Binns, R. W., 121, 124
Birbeck, H., 198
Birbeck, J., 190, 197
Birbeck, W., 42, 43, 50, 53, 103
Bir(k)beck, J., 25, 43
Birks, A., *Pls. 89, 90*; 103, 173-4
Birks, E., 198
Birks, L., *Pl. 82*; 103, 173, 174
Birks, Rawlins & Co., 174
Bloor, R., 68, 71
Boote, T., 151
Boote, Messrs. T. & R., 24, 151, 166
Bott, T., *Pls. 51, 52, 54, 56, 57*; 26, 122-3, 124-5, 139
Bott, T. J., 41, 43, 125, 139, 190, 197
Boullemier, A., *Pls. 43, 44, 47*; 28, 98-9, 103, 190, 197
Boullemier, H., 98-9
Boullemier, L., *Pl. 48*; 99, 103
Bourne (Coalport), 53
Bourne (Derby), 73, 76
Bourne, S., 103
Bowdler, A., 42, 43
Bowers, G. F., 24
Boyle, J, 89
Bradbury, R., 174
Bradley, J., 123, 139
Brameld, J. W., 24, 189
Brayford, (?), 53
Brecknell, J., 139
Brock, T., 139
Brough, C. B., 52, 53
Broughton, J., 76
Brown, W., 198
Brownfield, Messrs. W., 93, 174, 191
Brownfield's Guild Pottery, 191
Brown-Westhead, Moore, 29, 41, 99, 190-1
Bruff, C., 41
Bruff, P., 41
Buxton, S., 94, 103
B. W. M. mark, 199

C

Callowhill, J., *Pl. 60*; 123, 139
Callowhill, T., *Pls. 53, 60*; 123, 125, 139
Campbell, C. Minton, 93, 99
Carrara, 152
Carrier, A. E., 103, 164
Carrier de Belleuse, see Carrier, A. E.
Carrier-Belleuse, see Carrier, A. E.
Cartlidge, J., 54
Cauldon, see Ridgway and Brown-Westhead, Moore
Chamberlains (Worcester), *Pls. 49, 66*; 23, 120–1
Cheverton, B., 162–3
Chivers, F. H., 42, 139
Clarke, T., 71
Clementson, J., 24
Cloisonne style, 28
Coalbrookdale, 31
Coalport, *Pls. 1–11*; 23, 24, 25 and Chapter 2
    Artists, 42–4
    Marks, 44–5, 211
    Parian, 41 and Chapter 7
    Pattern numbers, 45–6
    Sèvres style, 31, 32
Cocker, D., 70–1
Cocker, G., 70, 76, 103
Cole, H., 194–5
Coleman, H. C., 97, 103
Coleman, R., 97, 103
Coleman, W. S., *Pl. 43*; 95–8, 103
Comelera, P., 103
Cook, W., *Pl. 8*; 23, 25, 40, 43
Cooper, W., 94, 103
Copeland, Messrs., *Pls. 15–23, 69, 76*; 21, 23, 24, 25, 26, 27, 28, 49–53, 196
    Artists, 53–4
    Marks, 66
    Parian, 49 and Chapter 7
    Pattern numbers, 67
Copeland, W. T., 47, 49
Copeland & Garrett, Messrs., *Pls. 12–14*; Chapter 3
    Marks, 65
    Parian, 47 and Chapter 7
    Pattern numbers, 67
Copson, O. H., 139
Corden, W., *Pl. 100*; 68–9
Crane, W., 103
Crook, J., 139
Crown Derby, see Derby
Crystal Palace Art-Union, 48, 150
Curnock, P., 193, 199

D

Daniell, Messrs. A. B. & R. P., 24, 25, 32, 176, 196, 210
Dating, General, Chapter 10
Davenport, Messrs., *Pl. 93*; 189-90, 200
Davenport Patent, 189, 200
Davies, E., 197
Davis, H., 139
Davis, J., 123, 139
Deakin, E., 24
Deakin, H., 76
Dean, J., 54
Dean, J. E., 100–1, 103
Dean, W. E. J., 75–76
Derby, *Pls. 24–30*; Chapter 4
    Artists, 75–7
    Bloor period, 68–71
    Crown Derby, 73–5
    King Street Works, 71–3, 75
    Marks, 71, 77–80
    Pattern numbers, 80
    Royal Crown Derby, 75
Dewsbury, D., 193, 199
Dexter, W., 68
Diamond shape mark, 209 and Appendix I
Dixon, T., 43
Dixon, W., 68
Dodson, R., 68
Doe, E., Junr., 140
Doe, E., Senr., 139
Donaldson, A. B., 98, 103
Doulton, Messrs., *Pls. 96, 98*; 193, 200
Dudley, M., 104
Duke, Sir J. & Nephews, 50, 191
Dutton, J., 197

E

Eaton, A., 199
Eaton, R., 43, 198
Earthenware, see subsequent volume in this series
Edwards, T., 197
Elden, M., 98, 104
Ellis, J., 191, 197
"England" marks, 210
Ermine mark, 94
Evans, D., *Pl. 12*; 23, 48–9, 54, 140
Evans, G., 140
Evans, J. B., 104
Evans, W., quoted, 49

INDEX

Exhibitions, Chapter I
  Manchester 1845-6, 19-21
  1851, *Pls. 6, 15, 16, 34, 36-8, 75-6*; 21-4
  1853, *Pl. 50*; 24, 122
  1855, 24-5, 122-3
  1862, *Pls. 9, 17, 39-42*; 25-6
  1867, 26
  1871, *Pls. 10, 56-7*; 27, 125
  1872, *Pl. 59*; 27
  1873, 27, 125
  1878, *Pl. 60*; 27-9, 127, 175
Exhibition, taste, 21-2
Eyre, G., 50, 54, 104, 191
Eyre, J., 54, 98, 104

F

Factory date cyphers
  Derby, 76-7
  Doulton, 200
  Mintons, 114-15
  Worcester (Royal), 142, 145
  Worcester (Grainger), 143-4
Fletcher, W., 198
Flight, Barr & Barr, 120
Foley, J. H., *Pl. 76*; 25, 149
Foster, H. W., 100-1, 104

G

Garrett, S., 151
Garrett, T., 47, 49
Gibson, J., *Pl. 69*; 148-9
Goode, Messrs. T., 26, 176, 187, 196, 210, 215
Goode, W. J., 104
Goss, W. H., 193
Grainger-Worcester, *Pls. 68, 85*; 23, 127-8, 143, 187, 196
Grainger, G. & Co., *Pls. 68, 85*; 23, 127-8, 143, 187, 196
Grainger, Lee & Co., 128, 143
Grainger, T., 127
Green, A., 94, 104
Greenaway, Kate, style of, *Pl. 62*; 127
Gregory, A., 75, 76, 104
Gresley, C., 75
Grey, G., 104
Griffin mark, 189

H

Hadley, J., *Pls. 58, 59, 60, 62, 63, 67*; 125-7, 137-8, 140, 144
Hadley, L., 137

Hadley ware, *Pl. 67*; 137-8, 144
Hall, A., 43
Halse, (?), 54
Hamilton & Moore, 190
Hammond, E., 98, 104
Hancock, F., 193, 199
Hancock, G., 89, 104
Hancock, H. S., 76
Hancock, S., 70-2, 151
Hand mark, 191
Harper, J., 43
Harrison, C., 191, 197
Hart, C., 193
Hartshorn(e), J., 41, 43
Haslem, J., *Pl. 24*; 68-9, 76
Hassall, T., 54
Heath, C., 104
Henk, C., 92, 104
Henk, J., 92, 104
Henri Deux ware, copies of, 28, 95, 175
H. H. initials, 174
Hillman, (?), 197
Hogg, H. W., 73, 76
Hogg, J., 74
Hollins, H., *Pl. 83*; 104, 173, 174
Holtzendorf, Count, 74, 76
Hopewell, J., 123, 140
Hopkins, C. B., 199
Howard, F., 42, 43
Howell & James, 97, 194
H. S. initials, 174
Hürten, C. F., *Pls. 18, 20*; 25, 26, 49-50, 54

I

Indian tree pattern, 42
Ingram, W. R., 73, 76

J

Jahn, L. H., *Pl. 40*; 25, 93-4, 104, 191
James Duke (Sir), & Nephews, 50, 191
"Japan" patterns, *Pl. 27*; 71, 73, 128, 189
Japanese styles, *Pls. 58, 59*; 27, 28, 51, 125-6
Jeannest, E., *Pl. 38*; 104, 164
Johnson, W., 197
Jones, (?), 76
Jones, C., 43
Jones, Messrs. G., *Pl. 87*; 187-8, 201
Jones, R. G., 196
J. R. & Co. mark, 190
J. W. R. mark, 190

K

Keeling, T., 43
Keene, (?), 74
Kelshall, (?), 43
Kerr & Binns, Messrs., *Pls. 50, 51, 52, 77*; 23, 24, 25, 26, 121-4
  Artists, 139-40
  Marks, 124, 141
Kerr, W. H., 121
Keys & Mountford, 167-8
King Street Works, Derby, *Pl. 26*; 71-3, 75
Kirk, W. B., *Pl. 77*; 122, 140
Kirkby, T., 93, 104

L

Lace work, 89-90
Landgraff, G., 73, 76, 191, 198
Larcombe, W., 72
Latham, J., 43, 94, 104
Lawrence, S., 43
Lawton, S., 140
L. B. initials, 174
Lead, L., 76
Lee, H., 54
Leger(e), (?), 191, 198
Leonce, G., 198
Leroy, D., *Pls. 30, 45*; 75, 76, 99, 104
Lessore, E., 93, 104
"Limoges" enamels, style of, *Pls. 51, 52, 56, 57*; 25, 26, 122-3, 124
Lithophanes, 195-6
Llanelly, 196
Locke & Co., 128, 137, 144
Locke, E., 128, 140, 187
Locker, W., 71, 75
Lockett, B., 104
Longmore, T., 104
Lucas, D., Junr., *Pls. 16, 17*; 23, 43, 50, 54
Lucas, D., Senr., 68-9, 76
Lunn, R., 74

M

McBirney, D., 192
"Made in England" mark, 210
Madeley, 39, 40
Magazine of Art, quoted, 73, 97, 100, 137
"Majolica" body, 91, 93, 102
Mallet, P., 198
Marks:
  Coalport, 44-5
  Copeland & Garrett, 65

Marks—*contd.*
  Copeland, 66
  Davenport, 200
  Derby, 77-80
  Doulton, 200
  Minton, 89, 94, 114-18
  Various, 164, 199-202
  Worcester, 124, 141-5
Marks, H. S., 104
Marsh, J., 198
Marshall, C., 192
Mason, (?), 43
Mason, Messrs. C., 24
Mayer, Messrs. T. J. & J., 24
M. & B. mark, 89
Meigh, C., 24, 168
Meli, G., 54, 191
Mellor, T., 104, 173
Micklewright, (?), 54
Miles, see Solon, M. L.
Minton(s), Messrs., *Pls. 31-48, 70-75, 79, 82-3, 86, 88-92*; 21, 22, 24, 26, 28, and Chapter 5, 151, 168-9, 170, 173-6, 194
  Artists, 103-4, 113-14
  London Studio, 97-8, 117
  Marks, 89, 94, 114-18
  Parian, *Pls. 33, 70-5, 79*; 89 and Chapter 7
  Pâte-sur-Pâte, *Pls. 82-92*; 27, 28, 95, 100, 164 and Chapter 8
  Pattern numbers, 118-19
Minton, H., *Pl. 79*; 89, 93
Minton Hollins, Messrs., 91
Minton, T., 89
Mitchell, H., 27, 94, 104, 193, 199
Moore, B., 190
Moore Brothers, Messrs., *Pls. 84, 94-5*; 95, 174, 176, 187, 190, 202
Moore, S., 190
Morgan, A., 104, 173
Morris, R. G., 73
Mortlock, J., 128, 196, 210
Mosley, W. E., 76
Mottershead, 43
Mountford, Jesse, *Pl. 99*; 43, 68, 189, 198
Mountford, John, 54, 151, 167-8
Mussill, W., 27, 99-100, 113

N

Nixon, G., 198
Nixon, H., 201
Noble, M., 25
Noke, C. J., 199

O

Owen, G., *Pl. 65*; 127, 140

P

Paget, F. H., 72
"Palissy" wares, 102
Palm, (?), 113
Palmer, E., 198
Palmere, C., 41, 43, 140
Parian, *Pls. 33, 69–81*; 19, 23, 24, and Chapter 7
    Copelands, *Pls. 69, 76*; 19, 23, 24, 25, 27, 147–62, 166–7
    Mintons, *Pls. 33, 70–5, 79*; 100, 116, 151–64, 168–9
    Worcester, *Pl. 77*; 124, 128, 163, 164
Parker, J., 43
Parker, W., 192
Pâte-sur-Pâte, *Pls. 82–92*; 27, 28, 95, 100, 128, 164 and Chapter 8
Pattern, J., 43
Pattern numbers, 210
    Coalport, 45–6
    Copeland & Garrett, 67
    Copeland, 67
    Derby, 80
    Doulton, 201
    Minton, 118–19
    Wedgwood, 202
    Worcester, 145
Pegg, W., 72
Penson, H. S., 100, 113
Perling, R., 123, 140
Perry, A., 42, 44, 54
Phillips, E., 73
Phillips, E. (Artist), 140
Pierced designs, *Pl. 65*; 121, 127, 128
Pilsbury, R., *Pl. 95*; 94, 95, 113, 190
Piper, H., 199
Plant, J. H., 42, 44, 199
Platts, J., 74, 76
Pope, S., 191, 198
Pottery Gazette, quoted, 40, 42, 48, 49, 72, 73, 100, 101, 127, 128, 151
Potts, 163
Powell, W., 140
Powell, Wm., 140
Pratt, Messrs. F. & R., 24
Pratt, H. L., 113
Prince, E., 76
Protat, H., 113, 164, 192
Pugh, W., 41
Pugin, A. W. N., 113

R

Raby, E., 140, 187, 193, 199
Randall, G., 113
Randall, J., *Pls. 4, 5, 10, 102*; 23, 39, 44
Randall, T. M., 39
Ranford, S., *Pl. 53*; 123, 125, 140
"Raphaelesque" porcelain, 26, 124
R. B. initials, 174
"R^d. No. . . .", 209 and Appendix I
Registration mark, 209 and Appendix I
Registration numbers, 209 and Appendix I
Reuter, E. G., 98, 100–1, 113
Rhead, F., 113, 173, 174, 191
Rice, T. H., 113, 173, 174
Ridgway, J., 24, 190
Ridgway & Abington, 190
Ridgway & Bates, *Pl. 97*
Rischgitz, E., 93, 113
Rivers, L., 113
R. & L. mark, 164
Roberts, E., 113
Robinson, J., 72
Robinson & Leadbetter, 164
Rockfort, J. D., 98
Rockingham, 24, 39, 189
Rogers, G., 139
Rose, John & Co., see Coalport
Rose, J., 31
Rose, W. F., 31, 41
Rouchard, F., 113
Rouse, C., 75
Rouse, J., Junr., 76
Rouse, J., Senr., *Pl. 29*; 25, 40, 44, 68, 72, 75
Rousseau, E., 170
Royal Crown Derby, see Derby
Royal Worcester, see Worcester
Rushton, J., *Pl. 55*; 123, 140

S

Sadler, T., 54
Sala, G. A., quoted, 28, 29, 127, 175, 191
Salt, (?), 54
Salter, E., 140
Sanders, H., *Pl. 84*; 113, 173, 174
Schenck, F., *Pl. 87*; 187, 198
Sèvres porcelain redecorated, 39
Sèvres style, *Pls. 4, 5, 15, 25, 34, 41, 48*; 22–3, 24, 31–2, 39, 40, 92, 93, 99
S. & H. mark, 71, 78
Sherriff, J., 123, 140
Sieffert, E., 191, 198

INDEX

Simpson, A., 113
Simpson, J., *Pl. 31*; 90–1, 113
Simpson, M., 91
Simpson, P., *Pl. 11*; 42, 44
Simpson, T. (Coalport), 42, 44
Simpson, T. H., *Pl. 101*; 94, 113
Simpson, W. P., 91
Slater, A., 94, 113
Slater, J., 113
Slater, J., 199
Slater, W., Junr., 192, 193, 198
Slater, W., Senr., 68, 69, 76, 198
Smith, J., *Pl. 32*; 54, 94, 113
Smith, M., 113
Society of Arts' Exhibitions, 20, 31
Solon, L. V., 101–2, 113
Solon, M. L., *Pls. 88, 91, 92*; 27, 28, 95, 100, 113, 170–6, 188, 197
Solon's apprentices, *Pl. 86*; 173–5
Sparkes, G., *Pl. 66*; 138, 144
Spode, J., 47
Statuary porcelain, see Parian
Steele, E., 68, 70, 114
Steele, H., 68, 70, 76
Steele, H., Junr., 198
Steele, T., Junr., 44, 68, 70
Steele, T., Senr., 68, 69–70, 76, 89, 114, 198
Stephen, (?), 73
Stephens, H., 44
Stevens, A., 114
Stevenson & Co., 71
Stevenson & Hancock, *Pl. 26*; 71
Stevenson, Sharp & Co., 71
Stewart, R., 114
Stinton, J., *Pl. 68*; 140
Summerly, Felix, 194–5
Summerly's Art Manufactures, *Pls. 70, 71*; 20, 21, 164, 194–5
Sutton, F., 140

T

Taylor, W., 140, 198
Thomas, J., 114
Thomason, J., 71
Toft, A., 95
Toft, C., 94, 95, 114, 140, 173, 175

Trevies, W., 44
Turner, A., 114

V

Victorian earthenware, see subsequent volume in this series

W

Wale, J. P., 77
Walklett, R., 114
Wallace, R., 54
Wareham, J., 94, 114
Waring, J. B., quoted, 25, 26, 50, 191
W. B. marks, 199
W. B. & S. marks, 199
Weaver, C., 52, 54
Weaver, J., 27, 52, 54, 123, 140
Webster, M., 68
Wedgwood, J. & Sons, 24, 92, 169, 174, 193–4, 202
Wells, L., 140
Wengers, Ltd., 216
White, G., *Pl. 96*; 193, 199
Whittaker, J., 70, 77
Williams, J. (Coalport), 44
Williams, J. (Worcester), 123, 140
Wilson, S., 193, 199
Winfield, R. W., 164
Wood, M., 25
Worcester
  Chamberlain, *Pls. 49, 66*; 23, 120–1, 141
  Kerr & Binns, *Pls. 50, 51, 52, 77*; 23, 24, 25, 26, 121–4, 141
  "Royal Worcester", *Pls. 53–65*; 26, 27, 28, 124–7
  Grainger, *Pls. 68, 85*; 127–8, 143–4
  Hadley, *Pl. 67*; 137–8, 144
  Locke, 128, 137, 144
Wornum, R. N., quoted, 22
Worrell, (?), 44
Wright, A. H., *Pl. 46*; 100–1, 114
Wyse, W., 114

Y

Yahn, see Jahn
Yale, W., *Pl. 22*; 52, 54